Importing from China

Other Books in the Current Controversies Series

Importing from China

Debra A. Miller, Book Editor

GREENHAVEN PRESS
A part of Gale, Cengage Learning

GALE
CENGAGE Learning™

Detroit • New York • San Francisco • New Haven, Conn • Waterville, Maine • London

Christine Nasso, *Publisher*
Elizabeth Des Chenes, *Managing Editor*

© 2009 Greenhaven Press, a part of Gale, Cengage Learning

Gale and Greenhaven Press are registered trademarks used herein under license.

For more information, contact:
Greenhaven Press
27500 Drake Rd.
Farmington Hills, MI 48331-3535
Or you can visit our Internet site at gale.cengage.com

For product information and technology assistance, contact us at

Gale Customer Support, 1-800-877-4253
For permission to use material from this text or product, submit all requests online at www.cengage.com/permissions

Further permissions questions can be emailed to permissionrequest@cengage.com

Articles in Greenhaven Press anthologies are often edited for length to meet page requirements. In addition, original titles of these works are changed to clearly present the main thesis and to explicitly indicate the author's opinion. Every effort is made to ensure that Greenhaven Press accurately reflects the original intent of the authors. Every effort has been made to trace the owners of copyrighted material.

Cover photograph © Ingram Publishing/Superstock.

LIBRARY OF CONGRESS CATALOGING-IN-PUBLICATION DATA

Importing from China / Debra A. Miller, book editor.
   p. cm. -- (Current controversies)
Includes bibliographical references and index.
ISBN 978-0-7377-4322-7 (hardcover)
ISBN 978-0-7377-4321-0 (pbk.)
1. United States--Commerce--China. 2. China--Commerce--United States. 3. Imports--United States. 4. Exports--China. 5. United States--Commercial policy.
I. Miller, Debra A.
   HF3128.I47 2009
   382'.0951073--dc22

                                                                    2008035442

Printed in the United States of America
1 2 3 4 5 6 7 12 11 10 09 08

Contents

Chapter 1: Does Trade with China Benefit the United States?

Yes: Trade with China Benefits the United States

No: Trade with China Does Not Benefit the United States

Chapter 2: Who Oversees the Quality and Safety of Chinese Imports?

Chapter 4: Should the United States Toughen Its Trade Policy Toward China?

Foreword

By definition, controversies are "discussions of questions in which opposing opinions clash" (*Webster's Twentieth Century Dictionary Unabridged*). Few would deny that controversies are a pervasive part of the human condition and exist on virtually every level of human enterprise. Controversies transpire between individuals and among groups, within nations and between nations. Controversies supply the grist necessary for progress by providing challenges and challengers to the status quo. They also create atmospheres where strife and warfare can flourish. A world without controversies would be a peaceful world; but it also would be, by and large, static and prosaic.

The Series' Purpose

The purpose of the *Current Controversies* series is to explore many of the social, political, and economic controversies dominating the national and international scenes today. Titles selected for inclusion in the series are highly focused and specific. For example, from the larger category of criminal justice, *Current Controversies* deals with specific topics such as police brutality, gun control, white collar crime, and others. The debates in *Current Controversies* also are presented in a useful, timeless fashion. Articles and book excerpts included in each title are selected if they contribute valuable, long-range ideas to the overall debate. And wherever possible, current information is enhanced with historical documents and other relevant materials. Thus, while individual titles are current in focus, every effort is made to ensure that they will not become quickly outdated. Books in the *Current Controversies* series will remain important resources for librarians, teachers, and students for many years.

In addition to keeping the titles focused and specific, great care is taken in the editorial format of each book in the series. Book introductions and chapter prefaces are offered to provide background material for readers. Chapters are organized around several key questions that are answered with diverse opinions representing all points on the political spectrum. Materials in each chapter include opinions in which authors clearly disagree as well as alternative opinions in which authors may agree on a broader issue but disagree on the possible solutions. In this way, the content of each volume in *Current Controversies* mirrors the mosaic of opinions encountered in society. Readers will quickly realize that there are many viable answers to these complex issues. By questioning each author's conclusions, students and casual readers can begin to develop the critical thinking skills so important to evaluating opinionated material.

Current Controversies is also ideal for controlled research. Each anthology in the series is composed of primary sources taken from a wide gamut of informational categories including periodicals, newspapers, books, U.S. and foreign government documents, and the publications of private and public organizations. Readers will find factual support for reports, debates, and research papers covering all areas of important issues. In addition, an annotated table of contents, an index, a book and periodical bibliography, and a list of organizations to contact are included in each book to expedite further research.

Perhaps more than ever before in history, people are confronted with diverse and contradictory information. During the Persian Gulf War, for example, the public was not only treated to minute-to-minute coverage of the war, it was also inundated with critiques of the coverage and countless analyses of the factors motivating U.S. involvement. Being able to sort through the plethora of opinions accompanying today's major issues, and to draw one's own conclusions, can be a complicated and frustrating struggle. It is the editors' hope that *Current Controversies* will help readers with this struggle.

Introduction

"How China accomplished [its] amazing economic revolution, whether it will succeed, and what it might mean for the United States and the rest of the world, has become one of the more fascinating topics of discussion among U.S. policymakers."

China has one of the fastest growing economies in the world. The Asian nation has changed from what many regarded as a backward, agrarian society into a formidable manufacturing center and global trader seemingly overnight. In fact, since China started its economic revolution in 1978, its economy has grown on average nearly ten percent each year, and its total foreign trade has soared from about $20.6 billion to more than $2.1 trillion in 2007, according to U.S. government statistics. In 2004, China overtook Japan as the world's third largest exporter, just behind Germany and the United States. Since then, the Chinese economy has continued to grow, and many experts maintain that China will soon replace the United States as the world's largest economic power, perhaps as early as 2020. How China accomplished this amazing economic transformation, whether it will succeed, and what it might mean for the United States and the rest of the world, has become one of the more fascinating topics of discussion among U.S. policymakers.

China's rapid economic rise can be traced back to a change of power in the early 1900s. For more than 2,000 years, China was ruled by a succession of dynasties in which the same family or group maintained power for generations. In 1911, however, Chinese revolutionaries overthrew the last dynasty, called the Manchu Dynasty, and the Republic of China was founded.

The fledgling government, however, faced great odds. Regional warlords competed for control in the vast country; foreign powers rushed in to take advantage of the weak national government; and famine, disease, and social violence were commonplace among the nation's 400 million people. Civil war soon erupted, and in 1937, just before the start of World War II, the Japanese took advantage of the unrest to invade and occupy China.

In 1949, however, China began to stabilize when the Chinese Communist party won the civil war and established China's current government—The People's Republic of China. The Communists approached the monumental problem of transforming a huge, poor, and divided population into an organized nation by imposing strict, sometimes ruthless, government control over most aspects of Chinese life. The Communist government eliminated threats posed by foreign interests and local militias, established a state-controlled economy, and implemented a national strategy that it called "Four Modernizations"—an ambitious program to modernize Chinese agriculture, industry, science and technology, and defense. China also implemented numerous cultural and political campaigns, such as the "Great Leap Forward," geared to indoctrinating the Chinese masses with the ideals of the ruling Communist party, with the goal that they would become loyal and self-sacrificing citizens.

By the late 1970s, Chinese leader Deng Xiaoping began to initiate modern economic reforms, marking China's entry into the global economic system. These reforms included loosening certain aspects of the government's control over the economy, introducing elements of a free-market system, and encouraging foreign investment. For example, the government began offering profit incentives and bonuses in place of political rewards for increases in production. Rural peasants were given greater decision-making power over agriculture, and factory managers in the cities were granted more flexibility in running operations. China also began to develop its rich natural resources, and it invited foreign experts and companies into the country to help with the development and modernization process. During this period, too, increasing numbers of Chinese students were sent abroad to pursue advanced degrees in various scientific and technical fields.

In 2001, China was admitted into the World Trade Organization (WTO), an international institution that sets and enforces global trade rules. This achievement has further accelerated China's economic growth, by opening many new markets for its exports. Today, China maintains a huge trade surplus, exporting many more goods than it imports. This is quite a feat, considering that it also has been importing and consuming an increasing amount of goods and raw materials in order to modernize its urban areas, infrastructure, and manufacturing industries. The country's economic success has begun to create a large middle class, though most Chinese still live at standards far below the rest of the industrialized world. China's low wages, however, have helped to keep Chinese goods competitively priced, further increasing foreign demand and contributing to the country's economic success.

The United States is China's top trading partner and its most important market. In 2007, for example, the United States imported Chinese goods worth more than $321 billion, according to figures released by the U.S. government. Chinese imports included a variety of products, but the three largest categories were toys and games, clothing, and electrical machinery and equipment. The United States also exports goods to China, but U.S. exports in 2007 amounted only to about $65 billion, creating a trade deficit for the United States with China of roughly $265 billion. At the same time, China has invested much of its trade surplus in U.S. treasury bonds and securities, making it one of our largest foreign creditors. Out of a total U.S. debt of more than $9 trillion, the United States owes China approximately $390 billion (surpassed only by Japan, which holds $580 billion of U.S. debt, and followed by the United Kingdom, to which the United States owes $320 billion).

The U.S.-China trading relationship is quite complex. Many experts point out that Chinese imports and investments have provided consumers with inexpensive products, kept U.S. interest rates low, and contributed to Americans' high standard of living for the past two decades. Others say that too many U.S. companies now manufacture their goods in China, taking good-paying jobs away from Americans, and that China's product quality standards are lax, as shown by the number of Chinese imports recently found to be unsafe or defective. Some policymakers also fear that China's creditor status gives it too much political leverage over the United States, because it could sell its vast holdings of U.S. bonds and treasury notes—an action that could devalue the U.S. currency (the dollar), raise interest rates, and spark a recession.

The differing views about whether U.S.-China trade is ultimately positive or negative for the United States are examined in *Current Controversies: Importing from China*. More specifically, the authors in this volume debate whether Chinese imports benefit the United States, whether imports are safe for U.S. consumers, whether the U.S.-China trade deficit is a threat, and what, if anything, should be done to alter U.S.-China trade relations.

CHAPTER 1

Does Trade with China Benefit the United States?

Chapter Preface

On December 11, 2001, China joined the World Trade Organization (WTO), an international organization that regulates global trade among its 43 member countries. The event was the culmination of fifteen years of negotiations that began in 1986, when China first applied for admission to the WTO's predecessor, the General Agreement on Tariffs and Trade (GATT). The negotiations largely involved complex issues of what tariffs, or taxes, would be applied on industrial and agricultural goods coming in and out of China, and how much China was prepared to open its markets to foreign products and services. For China, therefore, its WTO accession was a great victory. For the rest of the world, it was a signal that China intended to become a major player in the global economy.

Chinese officials hope that its WTO membership will help fuel China's continuing economic expansion by opening new markets, expanding trade, and increasing foreign investment. More money flowing into China, in turn, should bring more jobs, higher wages, and increased and better consumer choices for the Chinese people. WTO membership also is expected to give China the ability to participate in formulating the rules that regulate international trade and investment. Another benefit for China is that the WTO will provide a forum for resolving trade disputes and bring stability to China's trading system. Increased competition brought by more open trade, too, should help China to improve the quality of its products and the productivity of its manufacturing sector. Overall, participation in the WTO trading system should provide incentives for continued economic and legal reforms and help China to modernize and develop as a nation.

At the same time, WTO membership imposes significant responsibilities on China. The agreements China signed require it to undertake many difficult economic reforms, such as slashing its industrial and agricultural tariffs on foreign goods and opening its doors to various types of foreign services (such as banking, insurance, telecommunications, and professional services). China also agreed to reduce its subsidies for certain domestic products and to enact broad reforms, including government transparency, uniform application of laws, and increased judicial review. Other commitments made by China include abiding by WTO trade rules governing all aspects of global trade, such as those relating to intellectual property rights (that is, patents and other legal protections for product inventions), and adhering to various agreements made with individual WTO member countries. Some of these changes were required immediately, but others were to be made over a transition period of three to five years.

On December 11, 2006, China celebrated its first five years as a WTO member. Although a short period of time in economic terms, these five years have made clear that joining the WTO has been very good for China. China's embrace of its WTO commitments has quickly opened its economy to increased trade with many nations, and over this period its economy has almost doubled in size. China moved from being the world's sixth-largest trading nation to the third-largest. Its exports skyrocketed, and it has developed a record trading surplus. China also has benefited from a flood of foreign investment, and many countries are now eyeing China's growing middle class as a potentially explosive consumer market for all types of products. To showcase its new international status, China hosted the 2008 Olympic Games.

China's WTO performance during the past five years also has affected the rest of the world. Most commentators agree that, overall, even though it remains a non-democratic Communist country, China's record of WTO membership has proven that it is committed to market-driven economic reforms and to a path of full integration with the global economy. Its many structural economic changes have opened its markets to foreign imports and investment and given many international companies a source for low-cost manufacturing operations. From the perspective of the United States and many other countries, however, China's growth has brought both benefits and negative consequences.

In the United States, for example, cheap imports from China benefited U.S. consumers by keeping the costs of many products low. And many U.S. companies that have outsourced their manufacturing to China have benefited from China's low labor costs. Some experts argue, however, that China has drawn good-paying manufacturing jobs away from the United States. In addition, some Chinese products, such as toys and processed foods, have been shown to be unsafe or of poor quality. China's lax environmental policies and regulations and its disregard for intellectual property rights also have been seen as serious problems. Moreover, the U.S.-China trade deficit (that is, the large number of Chinese imports as compared with the relatively small number of U.S. exports to China) has grown so large during the past decade that some people worry that the U.S. economy is now dependent on this flow of cheap goods, giving China significant political and economic leverage over the United States. U.S. policymakers also have complained that China continues to adopt unfair trade practices that benefit the Chinese but block or penalize foreign exporters. For example, the United States complains that China has artificially kept the value of its currency, the yuan, low compared with the U.S. dollar—a situation that makes Chinese goods cheaper in the United States and U.S. goods more expensive in China, thus contributing to the large trade imbalance between the two countries.

The viewpoints in this chapter exemplify some of the differing opinions about whether China's entry onto the world trading stage has been beneficial or harmful to the United States.

China Has Not Been a Major Cause of U.S. Job Losses

Daniel T. Griswold

Daniel T. Griswold is director of the Cato Institute's Center for Trade Policy Studies and the author of a trade briefing paper titled "Who's Manipulating Whom? China's Currency and the U.S. Economy," from which this article is excerpted.

Everyone can agree that imports stamped "Made in China" have soared in the past decade. In 2005, imports from China reached $243.5 billion, a huge increase from the $38.8 billion in goods imported from China in 1994.

During that same period, imports from China as a share of total U.S. imports rose from six to 15%. Since 1994, imports from China have grown more than twice as fast as imports from the rest of the world.

Rising imports from China [of textile goods] have not so much replaced domestic production in the United States as they have replaced imports that used to come from other lower-wage countries.

Chinese Imports and U.S. Job Losses

Despite their rapid increase, imports from China have not been a major cause of job losses in the U.S. economy. Chinese manufacturers tend to specialize in lower-tech, labor-intensive goods, in contrast to the higher-tech, capital-intensive goods that are the comparative advantage of U.S. manufacturers.

For example, the apparel and footwear industries in the United States have been in decline for decades, long before China became a major exporter of those goods.

Daniel T. Griswold, "American Worry-Mongering About China," *The Globalist*, August 1, 2006. www.theglobalist.com. Daniel T. Griswold is director of the Center for Trade Studies at the Cato Institute in Washington, D.C. Copyright © 2000-2008 by *The Globalist*. Reproduced by permission.

Rising imports from China have not so much replaced domestic production in the United States as they have replaced imports that used to come from other lower-wage countries.

An Asian Manufacturing Chain

A key to understanding our trade relationship with China is to see China as the final assembly and export platform for a vast and deepening East Asian manufacturing supply chain.

Even in mid-range products such as personal computers, telephones and TVs, rising imports from China have typically displaced imports from other countries rather than domestic U.S. production.

Final products that Americans used to buy directly from Japan, South Korea, Taiwan, Hong Kong, Singapore and Malaysia are increasingly being put together in China with components from throughout the region.

China's more economically advanced neighbors typically make the most valuable components at home, ship them to China to be assembled with lower-value-added components, and then export the final product directly from China to the United States and other destinations.

Contrary to the often stated charge, imports from China are not the primary cause of the decline in U.S. manufacturing jobs.

As China imports more and more intermediate components from the region, its growing bilateral trade surplus with the United States has been accompanied by growing bilateral deficits with its East Asian trading partners.

While imports from China have been growing rapidly compared to overall imports, the relative size of imports from the rest of East Asia has been in decline. In 1994, the year China fixed its currency to the dollar, imports from East Asia accounted for 41% of total U.S. imports.

Today imports from that part of the world, including those from China, account for 34% of total U.S. imports. In other words, the rising share of imports from China has been more than offset by an even steeper fall in the share of imports from the rest of Asia.

The sharp rise in imports from China is not primarily driven by China's currency regime, but by its emergence as the final link in an increasingly intricate East Asian manufacturing supply chain.

The Real Cause of U.S. Job Losses

What about those three million lost manufacturing jobs? Contrary to the often stated charge, imports from China are not the primary cause of the decline in U.S. manufacturing jobs since 2000.

The primary reason why a net three million manufacturing jobs have disappeared since then is not imports from China, but the U.S. domestic recession of 2001, sluggish demand abroad for U.S. exports—and, most of all, soaring productivity gains by U.S. factories.

After rising rapidly during the 1990s, U.S. manufacturing output peaked and began to fall in the summer of 2000 as rising interest rates and energy prices began to tip the U.S. economy into recession.

The same recession in 2001 that hurt domestic manufacturing output also caused a 4.7% drop in the volume of imported manufactured goods that year. Meanwhile, sluggish growth abroad has hurt U.S. manufacturing exports.

An analysis by the President's [George W. Bush's] Council of Economic Advisors [CEA] determined that trade with China was not the primary cause of manufacturing job losses during the most recent recession.

"With the exception of apparel, the largest job losses have occurred in export-intensive industries for the United States, and job losses in U.S. manufacturing have been mainly industries in which imports from China are small," the CEA reported in the 2004 Economic Report of the President.

A Rise in U.S. Productivity

The main reason for declining employment in manufacturing, however, is the dramatic rise in productivity. Despite the painful recession in manufacturing from 2000 to 2003, real output of U.S. factories has still increased by 50% since 1994.

Because of productivity gains, manufacturing employment has been falling in a wide range of countries, including China itself.

American domestic manufacturers can produce so much more with fewer workers because remaining manufacturing workers are so much more productive.

Trade with China has probably accelerated the decline of more labor-intensive manufacturing sectors in the United States, such as footwear, apparel and other light manufacturing, but it has not caused a decline in total manufacturing output or capacity.

In fact, because of productivity gains, manufacturing employment has been falling in a wide range of countries, including China itself.

According to a 2003 study by Alliance Capital Management LP in New York, while the number of manufacturing workers in the United States dropped by 11% from 1995 through 2002, the number in China dropped even further—by 15%—or a net job loss of 15 million.

While Western companies were opening new factories in China, creating better paying jobs for Chinese workers, even more manufacturing workers were losing their jobs as old, inefficient state-owned enterprises went out of business.

The Insignificant Effects of Chinese Imports

Certainly some U.S. workers have lost their jobs because of America's expanding trade with China, but the number is not large compared to the total size of the U.S. labor force and the normal, healthy "churn" in the labor market.

Job losses caused by trade with China account for only about 1% of overall job displacement in the United States.

Even if one accepts the estimates of the critics of trade with China, the number of jobs eliminated because of Chinese imports would be in the neighborhood of 150,000 a year.

While not insignificant, that number is a small fraction of the number of people involuntarily displaced from their jobs each year in the United States, even during years of expansion and healthy job growth.

According to the U.S. Department of Labor, about 15 million jobs in the United States are permanently eliminated each year. In a related indicator, about 300,000 workers apply each week for unemployment insurance.

By either measure, job losses caused by trade with China account for only about 1% of overall job displacement in the United States.

Rather than impose trade sanctions in a misguided effort to save a small number of jobs lost each year because of trade with China, policymakers should focus on removing barriers to job creation, retraining and relocation to help those workers find new jobs being created in our dynamic economy.

The U.S.-China Trade Relationship Is Mutually Beneficial

Oxford Economics

Oxford Economics is an independently owned consulting company that provides economic advice, forecasts, and analytical tools to international institutions, governments, and blue-chip companies.

The dramatic expansion of trade and investment in services between China and United States has benefited both economies substantially and will continue to do so for the foreseeable future.

The expanding market for service-based jobs is vitally important to China's ability to absorb the large numbers of young workers and college graduates. . . .

The Importance of the Service Sector

In China, the service sector already is growing, contributing to economic development and a rise in living standards by boosting the productivity of industrial enterprises. The expanding market for service-based jobs is vitally important to China's ability to absorb the large numbers of young workers and college graduates entering the job market each year. Historically, the growth of a service sector also is seen as a significant step in the evolution of a nation's economy.

For the United States, which is the world's largest service economy, trade and investment in services with China trans-

Oxford Economics, "The Prospects for U.S.-China Services Trade and Investment: Executive Summary," *The China Business Forum*, December 2006. www.chinabusiness forum.org/pdf/us-china-services-trade-exsummary.pdf. © 2006 The China Business Forum. Reproduced by permission.

lates directly into high-wage US jobs and increased profits from investments in China that lead to further investment and job creation in the United States. The United States has a rapidly growing services trade surplus with China that slightly offsets the large manufacturing goods deficit. The more open the Chinese market for US service providers becomes, the more US services can be sold in China. These exports of services will continue to contribute positively to the US balance of payments.

From a broader perspective, the expansion of China's services infrastructure is essential to China's integration into the global economy and continued economic development. For example, China's establishment of a modern capital market will help China move toward a market-driven exchange rate. Market-based lending will help level the playing field between US and Chinese competitors. China's ability to provide pension and health care insurance to its citizens will enhance social stability and unlock capital resources tied up in precautionary savings. Improving the regulatory framework for services will help Chinese manufacturers and commercial firms to continue to move up the value chain, in all areas, from transportation, professional and financial services, and information technology, to retail, tourism, and hospitality, to name but a few.

These findings are the result of an extensive analysis of US-China services trade and investment conducted by Oxford Economics. The analysis demonstrates that China's initial implementation of its World Trade Organization (WTO) [an international organization that regulates global trade] commitments in services already benefits both economies. But even full implementation of these WTO commitments will leave in place a range of impediments to the growth of China's service sector, as well as service trade and foreign investment. By removing these constraints, both the Chinese and US economies will realize the full potential economic benefits of trade and investment in services detailed in this study.

Benefits for China

The United States is already a net exporter of a broad range of services to China: the United States had a services trade surplus with China of $2.6 billion in 2005.

- Chinese industry is growing rapidly in part because of strong imports of knowledge services, network services (transport, communication, and information technology) and financial services from developed economies.

- Oxford Economics estimates that the increase in China's service sector imports after 2001 resulted in higher average labor productivity of 0.3 percent. This productivity increase equates to an increase in Chinese GDP [gross domestic product, a measure of a country's economic output] of $6.5 billion. Of that, around $650 million is attributable to service sector imports from the United States.

- Higher production in Chinese industry means higher standards of living for millions of Chinese citizens—the goal of China's economic development plan.

- If the impediments to service sector growth in China are fully removed, the benefit would amount to an additional 2.5 percent of GDP ($138 billion in 2006 prices) by 2015. This would make the average Chinese household better off by $300 to $400, or RMB [renminbi, China's currency] 2,300 to RMB 3,100 per year. In comparison, average household income in China was around RMB 30,000 (around $3,700) in 2005. Service sector trade and investment flows with the United

States would generate one-tenth of the gains in household income by 2015 in this scenario.

- The growth in service sector trade and investment by 2015 will add up to 7 million jobs in China in relatively high-paying, high-productivity service industries if the impediments to service sector growth in China are fully removed.

Removing the remaining impediments to China's services market could boost US GDP by up to 0.2 percent, resulting in a permanent benefit for the entire US economy.

Benefits for the United States

- The United States is already a net exporter of a broad range of services to China: the United States had a services trade surplus with China of $2.6 billion in 2005. US service sector exports to China are growing rapidly—more rapidly than US service sector exports to any other economy. The United States is the world's largest exporter of services and is well positioned to benefit from China's rapidly growing demand for services.

- US service companies provide high-skill services to customers, employees, and markets throughout China, largely in knowledge, network, and financial service industries (including express delivery, banking, insurance, management consulting, and information technology services).

- US service sector net exports and net income of service sector investments to China, worth $3.1 billion in 2005, support some 37,000 jobs in high-productivity sectors of the US economy. This provides a permanent boost to US productivity—worth around $460 million in 2005.

- If the outstanding impediments to service sector growth in China are fully removed, the bilateral services trade surplus with China will increase to around $60 billion by 2015, supplemented by extra income derived from US service-related investments in China worth $7 billion. This would boost US GDP in the short term by about 0.3 percent.

- The average US household would be better off by about $500 per year in 2010 as a result of this growth in services trade with China.

- The significant and growing US current account surplus in services with China (including repatriated [repatriating is the process of converting a foreign currency into the currency of one's own country] profits from service sector foreign direct investment) is supporting the growth in service sector employment in the United States. The removal of all impediments to growth in services trade and investment with China would create up to 240,000 high-paying US service sector jobs by 2015.

- In the long run, removing the remaining impediments to China's services market could boost US GDP by up to 0.2 percent, resulting in a permanent benefit for the entire US economy. By 2050, US service sector exports to China could reach between 1.5 percent and 3.5 percent of US GDP. The US surplus on service sector trade with China could be worth around 1 percent of GDP, while inflows of profits from US service sector investments in China could contribute a further 0.5 percent of GDP to the US current account of the balance of payments.

Realizing These Benefits

This study makes clear that the benefits of service sector trade and investment accrue to both economies. Implementing fully China's WTO commitments is an essential first step to maximizing the advantages for both economies of service sector links. Implementation is well under way, and both economies will reap the substantial benefits in the years to come.

But greater benefits will be realized in both China and the United States if PRC [People's Republic of China] regulations, implementing rules, and license approvals are adjusted to increase the pace and scope of service sector reform.

In practice, this would entail:

- Increasing the transparency of the regulatory environment for foreign service providers, through early publication of proposed regulations, consultation with foreign and domestic industry, participation in international service sector forums, and adoption of international standards and norms

- Progressively deregulating markets for the provision of services, to encourage the growth of those services

- Addressing current restrictions on market access and expansion (including foreign ownership, industry, and geographic limitations) so that foreign expertise in the service sector can become another tool to further China's Five-Year Plan objectives

- Creating a level playing field, by reducing government support for domestic enterprises in the services markets

- Continuing to gather and publicize sectoral data about the performance of the Chinese economy, to enable all participants in the economy to understand more clearly how quickly the various service sectors in China are growing, and what their future growth prospects might be

Adopting such measures would generate significant benefits for China and the United States, helping China to move more quickly and effectively to achieve its own economic development goals.

Advantages of Trade with China Outweigh the Disadvantages

Craig K. Elwell and Marc Labonte

Craig K. Elwell and Marc Labonte are specialists in macroeconomics who work in the Government and Finance Division of the Congressional Research Service, a federal department established by Congress to provide authoritative, confidential, objective, and nonpartisan analysis on policy issues.

Is China a Threat to the U.S. Economy?

The rise of China from a poor, stagnant country to a major economic power within a time span of only 28 years is often described by analysts as one of the greatest economic success stories in modern times. Prior to 1979, China maintained a Soviet-style command economy under which the state controlled most aspects of the economy. These policies kept the economy relatively stagnant and living standards quite low. However, beginning in 1979, the government began a series of free market reforms and began opening up to the world in terms of trade and investment. These reforms have produced dramatic results. From 1979 to 2005, China's real gross domestic product (GDP) [a measure of a country's economic output] grew at an average annual rate of 9.7%, the size of its economy increased over 11-fold, its real per capita GDP grew over 8-fold, and its world ranking for total trade rose from 27th to 3rd.

Benefits to the United States

China's economic reforms and growth have benefited (or could benefit) the U.S. economy in a number of ways:

Craig K. Elwell and Marc Labonte, "CRS Report to Congress: Is China a Threat to the U.S. Economy?" Congressional Research Service, January 23, 2007. http://fpc.state.gov/documents/organization/81360.pdf. Reproduced by permission.

- Over the past few years, China has been the fastest growing U.S. export market among its major trading partners. For example, U.S. exports to China in 2006 increased by an estimated 33%. China's ranking as a U.S. export market rose from 11th in 2000 to 4th in 2006, and may overtake Japan in 2007 to become 3rd. [By the end of 2007, China did exceed Japan to become the 3rd export market.] China's rapid economic growth, coupled with its large population and development needs, makes it a potentially huge market for the United States.

- China has become the second-largest source for U.S. imports. In many instances, China has replaced other East Asian nations as a source for many manufactured products imported by the United States. Low-cost imports from China have helped restrain inflation and increased the purchasing power of U.S. consumers, and boosted demand for other products. This has helped U.S. production to shift into areas where the United States has a comparative advantage.

- China has become the second-largest purchaser of U.S. Treasury securities. These purchases have helped to fund the U.S. federal budget deficit and keep interest rates relatively low.

Concerns About China

In the near future, China will replace the United States as the world's largest economy and exporter.

At the same time, however, China's emergence as an economic power has raised a number of concerns among some Members of Congress who perceive China as a threat, or potential threat, to the U.S. economy. As one Member stated, "China's competitive challenge makes Americans nervous.

From Wall Street to Main Street, Americans are nervous about China's effect on the American economy, American jobs, on the American way of life." Areas of concern include the following issues:

- Analysts project that in the near future, China will replace the United States as the world's largest economy and exporter. In this context, China's economic rise is viewed as America's decline.

- The surge in U.S. imports from China is viewed by many as a threat to various U.S. economic sectors, particularly in manufacturing. China's nearly unlimited pool of low-cost labor is viewed by some as a serious competitive threat to U.S. manufacturing and is blamed for bankruptcies and/or plant relocation to China, job losses, and stagnant U.S. wages. This process could get worse as China begins to manufacture more advanced products that compete directly with those made by U.S. domestic firms.

- Many are concerned that China employs a number of unfair economic policies intended to benefit its economy at the expense of its trading partners, such as the United States. Many policymakers view the large and growing trade imbalance with China as proof that China does not trade fairly. They contend, for example, that China's policy of pegging its currency to the U.S. dollar is a deliberate policy meant to make Chinese exports relatively cheap in world markets, while discouraging imports. They also contend that China uses industrial policies (such as subsidies) and other unfair trade practices (such as dumping) to promote the development of various industries (such as autos and steel) deemed important to national development, which undermines the ability of U.S. firms in these sectors to compete in global markets, including the domestic U.S. market. In many respects, the rise of China as a global economic power is subject to the same interpretation as the economic rise of Japan during the 1970s and 1980s and the impact that rise was thought to have on the U.S. economy.

- Analysts describe a number of negative consequences of China's rapid economic growth, such as increasing demand for oil and raw materials (which drives up their prices) and growing pollution (which could have global implications). In addition, the lack of an effective intellectual property rights (IPR) enforcement regime has led to widespread IPR piracy in China. Not only does such piracy greatly diminish China as a market for IPR-related industries (such as music and software), such industries are further harmed by China's export of pirated products.

- Some analysts have raised concern over the possible consequences if China decided to reduce its large holdings of U.S. Treasury securities. Others worry about the potential effect of Chinese state-owned companies' attempts to purchase U.S. firms. . . .

Challenges and Opportunities

Although China will likely become the world's largest economy within the next decade or two, its living standards will remain substantially below those in the United States for several decades to come. . . . China's economic ascendancy will not in and of itself undermine or lower U.S. living standards—these will be largely determined by U.S. economic policies. In addition, although various Chinese economic policies may have negative effects on certain U.S. economic sectors, other U.S. sectors (as well as consumers) have benefited, and thus far the overall impact of China's economic growth and opening up to the world appears to have been positive for both the U.S. and Chinese economies.

From an economic perspective, describing China's economic rise or its economic policies as an economic "threat" to the United States fails to reflect the complex nature of the economic relationship and growing economic integration that is taking place. Hence it may be more accurate to say that China's economic growth poses both challenges and opportunities for the United States.

Trade with China Costs American Jobs

Robert E. Scott

Robert E. Scott is a senior international economist and director of international programs at the Economic Policy Institute, a nonprofit, nonpartisan think tank whose mission is to seek solutions that will result in broadly shared prosperity and opportunities for U.S. citizens.

Contrary to the predictions of its supporters, China's entry into the World Trade Organization (WTO) [an international organization that regulates global trade] has failed to reduce its trade surplus with the United States or increase overall U.S. employment. The rise in the U.S. trade deficit with China between 1997 and 2006 has displaced production that could have supported 2,166,000 U.S. jobs. Most of these jobs (1.8 million) have been lost since China entered the WTO in 2001. Between 1997 and 2001, growing trade deficits displaced an average of 101,000 jobs per year, or slightly more than the total employment in Manchester, New Hampshire. Since China entered the WTO in 2001, job losses increased to an average of 353,000 per year—more than the total employment in greater Akron, Ohio. Between 2001 and 2006, jobs were displaced in every state and the District of Columbia. Nearly three-quarters of the jobs displaced were in manufacturing industries. Simply put, the promised benefits of trade liberalization with China have been unfulfilled.

An Imbalanced Trade Relationship

As a matter of policy, China tightly pegs its currency's value to that of the dollar at a rate that encourages a large bilateral surplus with the United States. Maintaining this peg required

Robert E. Scott, "Costly Trade with China: Millions of U.S. Jobs Displaced with Net Job Loss in Every State," *Economic Policy Institute*, October 9, 2007. www.epi.org/content.cfm/bp188. Copyright © 2008 by The Economic Policy Institute. All rights reserved. Reproduced by permission.

the purchase of about $200 billion in U.S. Treasury Bills and other securities in 2006 alone. This intervention makes the yuan [Chinese dollar] artificially cheap and provides an effective subsidy on Chinese exports; best estimates are that the rate of this effective subsidy is roughly 40%. China also engages in extensive suppression of labor rights; it has been estimated that wages in China would be 47% to 85% higher in the absence of labor repression. China has also been accused of massive direct subsidization of export production. Finally, it maintains strict, non-tariff barriers to imports.

As a result, China's exports to the United States of $288 billion in 2006 were *six times greater* than U.S. exports to China, which were only $52 billion. China's trade surplus was responsible for 42.6% of the United States' total, non-oil trade deficit. This is by far the United States' most imbalanced trading relationship. Unless and until China revalues (raises) the yuan and eliminates these other trade distortions, the U.S. trade deficit and job losses will continue to grow rapidly in the future.

Major findings of [a study by the Economic Policy Institute, an economic think tank, showed:]

- The 1.8 million job opportunities lost nationwide since 2001 are distributed among all 50 states and the District of Columbia, with the biggest losers, in numeric terms: California (−269,300), Texas (−136,900), New York (−105,900), Illinois (−79,900), Pennsylvania (−78,200), North Carolina (−77,200), Florida (−71,900), Ohio (−66,100), Georgia (−60,400), and Massachusetts (−59,300).

- The 10 hardest-hit states, as a share of total state employment, are: New Hampshire (−13,000, −2.1%), North Carolina (−77,200, −2.0%), California (−269,300, −1.8%), Massachusetts (−59,300, −1.8%), Rhode Island (−8,400, −1.8%), South Carolina

(−29,200, −1.6%), Vermont (−4,900, −1.6%), Oregon (−25,700, −1.6%), Indiana (−45,200, −1.5%), and Georgia (−60,400, −1.5%).

China's entry into the WTO was supposed to . . . require that it open its markets to imports from the United States and other nations.

False Promises About China's Entry into the WTO

China's entry into the WTO was supposed to bring it into compliance with an enforceable, rules-based regime, which would require that it open its markets to imports from the United States and other nations. The United States also negotiated a series of special safeguard measures designed to limit the disruptive effects of surging Chinese imports on domestic producers. However, the core of the agreement failed to include any protections to maintain or improve labor or environmental standards. As a result, China's entry into the WTO has further tilted the international economic playing field against domestic workers and firms, and in favor of multinational companies (MNCs) from the United States and other countries, and state- and privately-owned exporters in China. This has increased the global "race to the bottom" in wages and environmental quality and caused the closing of thousands of U.S. factories, decimating employment in a wide range of communities, states, and entire regions of the United States.

Proponents of China's entry into the WTO frequently claimed that it would create jobs in the United States, increase U.S. exports, and improve the trade deficit with China. President [Bill] Clinton claimed that the agreement allowing China into the WTO, which was negotiated during his administration, "creates a win-win result for both countries." He argued that exports to China "now support hundreds of thousands of

American jobs" and that "these figures can grow substantially with the new access to the Chinese market the WTO agreement creates." Others in the White House, such as Kenneth Liberthal, the special advisor to the president and senior director for Asia affairs at the National Security Council, echoed Clinton's assessment: "Let's be clear as to why a trade deficit might decrease in the short term. China exports far more to the U.S. than it imports [from] the U.S. . . . It will not grow as much as it would have grown without this agreement and over time clearly it will shrink with this agreement."

Promises about jobs and exports misrepresented the real effects of trade on the U.S. economy: trade both creates and destroys jobs. Increases in U.S. exports tend to create jobs in the United States, but increases in imports tend to destroy jobs as imports displace goods that otherwise would have been made in the United States by domestic workers.

Between 2001 and 2006, after China entered the WTO, the deficit increased $30 billion per year on average.

The impact of changes in trade on employment is estimated . . . by calculating the labor content of changes in the trade balance—the difference between exports and imports. Each $1 billion in computer exports to China from the United States supports American jobs. However, each $1 billion in computer imports *from* China displaces those American workers, who would have been employed making them in the United States. On balance, the net employment effect of trade flows depends on the growth in the trade deficit; not just exports. Another critically important promise made by the promoters of liberalized U.S.-China trade was that the United States would benefit because of increased exports to a large and growing consumer market in China. This market, in turn, was to be based on an expansion of the middle class that, it was claimed, would grow rapidly due to the wealth created in

China by its entry into the WTO. However; the increase in U.S. exports to China has been overwhelmed by the growth of U.S. imports. . . .

Growing Trade Deficits and Job Losses

The U.S. trade deficit with China has increased from $50 billion in 1997 to $235 billion in 2006, an increase of $185 billion. . . . Between 1997 and 2001, prior to China's entry into the WTO, the deficit increased $9 billion per year on average. Between 2001 and 2006, after China entered the WTO, the deficit increased $30 billion per year on average.

While it is true that exports support jobs in the United States, it is equally true that imports displace them. The net effect of trade flows on employment must look at the trade balance. . . .

U.S. exports to China in 1997 supported 138,000 jobs, but U.S. imports displaced production that would have supported 736,000 jobs. . . . Therefore, the $49 billion trade deficit in 1997 displaced 736,300 jobs in that year. Job displacement rose to 1,000,000 jobs in 2001 and 2,763,000 in 2006. Prior to China's entry into the WTO, an average of 101,000 jobs per year were displaced by growing trade deficits between 1997 and 2001. After 2001, an average of 353,000 jobs per year were lost.

Growth in trade deficits with China has reduced demand for goods produced in every region of the United States and has led to job displacement in all 50 states and the District of Columbia. . . . More than 100,000 jobs were lost in California, Texas, and New York each. Jobs displaced due to growing deficits with China equaled or exceeded 2.0% of total employment in states such as North Carolina and New Hampshire. . . .

Growing trade deficits with China have clearly reduced domestic employment in traded goods industries, especially in the manufacturing sector, which has been hard hit by plant closings and job losses. Workers displaced by trade from the manufacturing sector have been shown to have particular difficulty in securing comparable employment elsewhere in the economy. More than one-third of workers displaced from manufacturing drop out of the labor force. Average wages of those who secured re-employment fell 11% to 13%. Trade-related job displacement pushes many workers out of good jobs in manufacturing and other trade-related industries, often into lower-paying industries and frequently out of the labor market. . . .

The Effect of Foreign Investments

Administration officials and other economists have argued that the capital inflow [from China's purchase of U.S. treasury notes and other securities] that is the mirror-image of trade deficits supports jobs in the United States by keeping interest rates lower than they would be absent this inflow. During the late 1990s, for example, these capital inflows fought rising trade deficits to a draw in terms of aggregate employment effects, and, through much of the 2000s recovery, interest-sensitive industries (housing and construction, for example) have surely expanded more than they would have absent foreign capital inflows. While these claims may be correct from a simple accounting standpoint, they do not support assertions that trade flows are a useless indicator of job loss.

The growing U.S. trade deficit with China has displaced huge numbers of jobs in the United States.

First, and most simply, it is just not true that foreign capital inflows always make up trade-induced employment losses one-for-one. In the 2001 recession and the jobless recovery following, growing trade deficits accompanied aggregate job loss, even as interest rates scraped historical bottoms. Clearly, low interest rates do not always translate into enough growth in investment and consumption in interest-sensitive sectors to always sterilize the impact of growing trade deficits.

Second, the job-loss numbers ... are a good measure of just how unbalanced the U.S. economy has become due to rising trade deficits. Tradable goods industries have hemorrhaged jobs, while interest-sensitive, often non-tradable, industries have seen rapid growth. At that point in the future when trade deficits begin to close, the U.S. economy will need to return many of the jobs displaced by rising trade deficits out of non-tradable and into tradable industries. Moving millions of workers back and forth between sectors is no mean trick, and accomplishing it without a recession in between will be hard; trying to do it after another couple of years of deficit growth—and an even more lopsided U.S. economy—will be even harder.

In short, while aggregate employment in the United States may well not respond job-for-job with the numbers reported in this paper on trade deficits with China, these numbers provide insight into how much harder other macroeconomic influences have to work to eliminate the employment drag from these deficits, and they provide a good (and ominous) measure of how lopsided employment growth in the U.S. economy has become owing to the unbalanced U.S.-China trade relationship.

Bad for Both Countries

The growing U.S. trade deficit with China has displaced huge numbers of jobs in the United States, and been a prime contributor to the crisis in manufacturing employment over the past six years. The current U.S.-China trade relationship is bad for both countries. The United States is piling up foreign debt, losing export capacity, and facing a more fragile macroeconomic environment.

Meanwhile, China has become dependent on the U.S. consumer market for employment generation, has suppressed the purchasing power of its own middle class with a weak currency, and, most importantly, has held hundreds of billions of hard-currency reserves in low-yielding, risky assets, instead of investing them in public goods that could benefit Chinese households. Its repression of labor rights has suppressed wages, thus subsidizing its exports and making them artificially cheap. This relationship needs a fundamental change: addressing the exchange rate policies and labor standards issues in the Chinese economy are important first steps.

U.S. Trade Imbalance with China Is Unsustainable

James Fallows

James Fallows is a national correspondent for The Atlantic Monthly *and past winner of the National Magazine Award and the National Book Award for nonfiction.*

Through the quarter-century in which China has been opening to world trade, Chinese leaders have deliberately held down living standards for their own people and propped them up in the United States. This is the real meaning of the vast trade surplus—$1.4 trillion and counting, going up by about $1 billion per day—that the Chinese government has mostly parked in U.S. Treasury notes. In effect, every person in the (rich) United States has over the past 10 years or so borrowed about $4,000 from someone in the (poor) People's Republic of China. Like so many imbalances in economics, this one can't go on indefinitely, and therefore won't. But the way it ends—suddenly versus gradually, for predictable reasons versus during a panic—will make an enormous difference to the U.S. and Chinese economies over the next few years, to say nothing of bystanders in Europe and elsewhere.

Any economist will say that Americans have been living better than they should—which is by definition the case when a nation's total consumption is greater than its total production, as America's now is. Economists will also point out that, despite the glitter of China's big cities and the rise of its billionaire class, China's people have been living far worse than they could. That's what it means when a nation consumes only half of what it produces, as China does.

James Fallows, "The $1.4 Trillion Question," *The Atlantic Monthly*, January/February 2008. www.theatlantic.com/doc/200801/fallows-chinese-dollars. Reproduced by permission of the author.

Concerns About the U.S.-China Imbalance

Neither government likes to draw attention to this arrangement, because it has been so convenient on both sides. For China, it has helped the regime guide development in the way it would like—and keep the domestic economy's growth rate from crossing the thin line that separates "unbelievably fast" from "uncontrollably inflationary." For America, it has meant cheaper iPods, lower interest rates, reduced mortgage payments, a lighter tax burden. But because of political tensions in both countries, and because of the huge and growing size of the imbalance, the arrangement now shows signs of cracking apart.

In an article two and a half years ago . . . [July 2005], I described an imagined future in which a real-estate crash and shakiness in the U.S. credit markets led to panic by Chinese and other foreign investors, with unpleasant effects for years to come. The real world has recently had inklings of similar concerns. . . . Relative nobodies in China's establishment were able to cause brief panics in the foreign-exchange markets merely by hinting that China might stop supplying so much money to the United States. In August [2007], an economic researcher named He Fan, who works at the Chinese Academy of Social Sciences and did part of his doctoral research at Harvard, suggested in an op-ed piece in *China Daily* that if the U.S. dollar kept collapsing in value, China might move some of its holdings into stronger currencies. This was presented not as a threat but as a statement of the obvious, like saying that during a market panic, lots of people sell. The column quickly provoked alarmist stories in Europe and America suggesting that China was considering the "nuclear option"—unloading its dollars.

A few months later, a veteran Communist Party politician named Cheng Siwei suggested essentially the same thing He Fan had. Cheng, in his mid-70s, was trained as a chemical engineer and has no official role in setting Chinese economic policy. But within hours of his speech, a flurry of trading forced the dollar to what was then its lowest level against the euro and other currencies. The headline in the *South China Morning Post* [a Chinese newspaper] the next day was: "Officials' Words Shrivel U.S. Dollar." Expressing amazement at the markets' response, Carl Weinberg, chief economist at the High Frequency Economics advisory group, said, "This would be kind of like Congressman Charlie Rangel giving a speech telling the Fed to hike or cut interest rates." In the following weeks, phrases like "run on the dollar" and "collapse of confidence" showed up more and more frequently in financial newsletters. The nervousness only increased when someone who does have influence, Chinese Premier Wen Jiabao, said last November [2007], "We are worried about how to preserve the value" of China's dollar holdings.

Effects of a Weakening U.S. Currency

When the dollar is strong, the following (good) things happen: the price of food, fuel, imports, manufactured goods, and just about everything else goes down. The value of the stock market, real estate, and just about all other American assets goes up. Interest rates go down—for mortgage loans, credit-card debt, and commercial borrowing. Tax rates can be lower, since foreign lenders hold down the cost of financing the national debt. The only problem is that American-made goods become more expensive for foreigners, so the country's exports are hurt.

When the dollar is weak, the following (bad) things happen: the price of food, fuel, imports, and so on (no more vacations in Europe) goes up. The value of the stock market, real estate, and just about all other American assets goes down. Interest rates are higher. Tax rates can be higher, to cover the increased cost of financing the national debt. The only benefit is that American-made goods become cheaper for foreigners, which helps create new jobs and can raise the value of export-oriented American firms.

Americans sometimes debate ... whether in principle it is good to rely so heavily on money controlled by a foreign government.

The dollar's value has been high for many years—unnaturally high, in large part because of the implicit bargain with the Chinese. Living standards in China, while rising rapidly, have by the same logic been unnaturally low. To understand why this situation probably can't go on, and what might replace it—via a dollar crash or some other event—let's consider how this curious balance of power arose and how it works.

China's U.S. Investments

By 1996, China amassed its first $100 billion in foreign assets, mainly held in U.S. dollars. By 2001, that sum doubled to about $200 billion, according to Edwin Truman of the Peterson Institute for International Economics in Washington. Since then, it has increased more than sixfold, by well over a trillion dollars, and China's foreign reserves are now the largest in the world. China's U.S. dollar assets probably account for about 70 percent of its foreign holdings, according to the latest analyses by Brad Setser, a former Treasury Department economist now with the Council on Foreign Relations; the rest are mainly in euros, plus some yen. Most of China's U.S. investments are in conservative, low-yield instruments like Treasury notes and federal-agency bonds. . . . Because notes and bonds backed by the U.S. government are considered the safest investments in the world, they pay lower interest than corporate bonds, and for the past two years their annual interest payments of 4 to 5 percent have barely matched the 5-to-6-percent decline in the U.S. dollar's value versus the RMB [renminbi, China's currency].

Americans sometimes debate (though not often) whether in principle it is good to rely so heavily on money controlled by a foreign government. The debate has never been more relevant, because America has never before been so deeply in debt to one country. Meanwhile, the Chinese are having a debate of their own—about whether the deal makes sense for them. Certainly China's officials are aware that their stock purchases prop up 401(k) values, their money-market holdings keep down American interest rates, and their bond purchases do the same thing—plus allow our government to spend money without raising taxes.

Some Chinese people are rich, but China as a whole is unbelievably short on many of the things that qualify countries as fully developed.

"From a distance, this, to say the least, is strange," Lawrence Summers, the former treasury secretary and president of Harvard, told me last year in Shanghai. He was referring to the oddity that a country with so many of its own needs still unmet would let "this $1 trillion go to a mature, old, rich place from a young, dynamic place."

It's more than strange. Some Chinese people are rich, but China as a whole is unbelievably short on many of the things that qualify countries as fully developed. Shanghai has about the same climate as Washington, D.C.—and its public schools have no heating. Beijing is more like Boston. On winter nights, thousands of people mass along the curbsides of major thoroughfares, enduring long waits and fighting their way onto hopelessly overcrowded public buses that then spend hours stuck on jammed roads. And these are the showcase cities! In rural Gansu province, I have seen schools where 18 junior-high-school girls share a single dormitory room, sleeping shoulder to shoulder, sardine-style.

Better schools, more-abundant parks, better health care, cleaner air and water, better sewers in the cities—you name it, and if it isn't in some way connected to the factory-export economy, China hasn't got it, or not enough. This is true at the personal level, too. The average cash income for workers in a big factory is about $160 per month. On the farm, it's a small fraction of that. Most people in China feel they are moving up, but from a very low starting point.

China's High Savings Rate

So why is China shipping its money to America? An economist would describe the oddity by saying that China has by far the highest national savings in the world. This sounds admirable, but when taken to an extreme—as in China—it indicates an economy out of sync with the rest of the world, and one that is deliberately keeping its own people's living standards lower than they could be. For comparison, India's savings rate is about 25 percent, which in effect means that India's people consume 75 percent of what they collectively produce. (The savings rate is the net share of national output either exported or saved and invested for consumption in the future. Effectively, it's what your own people produce but don't use.) For Korea and Japan, the savings rate is typically from the high 20s to the mid-30s. Recently, America's has at times been below zero, which means that it consumes, via imports, more than it makes.

China's savings rate is a staggering 50 percent, which is probably unprecedented in any country in peacetime. This doesn't mean that the average family is saving half of its earnings—though the personal savings rate in China is also very high. Much of China's national income is "saved" almost invisibly and kept in the form of foreign assets. Until now, most Chinese have willingly put up with this, because the economy has been growing so fast that even a suppressed level of consumption makes most people richer year by year.

But saying that China has a high savings rate describes the situation without explaining it. Why should the Communist Party of China countenance a policy that takes so much wealth from the world's poor, in their own country, and gives it to the United States? To add to the mystery, why should China be content to put so many of its holdings into dollars, knowing that the dollar is virtually guaranteed to keep losing value against the RMB? And how long can its people tolerate being denied so much of their earnings, when they and their country need so much? The Chinese government did not explicitly set out to tighten the belt on its population while offering cheap money to American homeowners. But the fact that it does results directly from explicit choices it *has* made—two in particular. Both arise from crucial controls the government maintains over an economy that in many other ways has become wide open. . . .

The U.S. and Chinese governments are always disagreeing—about trade, foreign policy, the environment. Someday the disagreement could be severe.

One is to dictate the RMB's value relative to other currencies, rather than allow it to be set by forces of supply and demand, as are the values of the dollar, euro, pound, etc. The obvious reason for doing this is to keep Chinese-made products cheap, so Chinese factories will stay busy. This is what Americans have in mind when they complain that the Chinese government is rigging the world currency markets. . . .

The other major decision is not to use more money to address China's needs directly—by building schools and agricultural research labs, cleaning up toxic waste, what have you. Both decisions stem from the central government's vision of what is necessary to keep China on its unprecedented path of growth. The government doesn't want to let the market set the value of the RMB, because it thinks that would disrupt the constant growth and the course it has carefully and expensively set for the factory-export economy. . . .

A Balance of Terror

Let's take [the] fears about a rich, strong China to their logical extreme. The U.S. and Chinese governments are always disagreeing—about trade, foreign policy, the environment. Someday the disagreement could be severe. Taiwan, Tibet, North Korea, Iran—the possibilities are many, though Taiwan always heads the list. Perhaps a crackdown within China. Perhaps another accident, like the U.S. bombing of China's embassy in Belgrade nine years ago, which everyone in China still believes was intentional and which no prudent American ever mentions here.

Would the Chinese use [their holdings in U.S. debt as a] weapon? The reasonable answer is no, because they would wound themselves grievously, too.

Whatever the provocation, China would consider its levers and weapons and find one stronger than all the rest—one no other country in the world can wield. Without China's billion dollars a day, the United States could not keep its economy stable or spare the dollar from collapse.

Would the Chinese use that weapon? The reasonable answer is no, because they would wound themselves grievously, too. Their years of national savings are held in the same dollars that would be ruined; in a panic, they'd get only a small share out before the value fell. Besides, their factories depend on customers with dollars to spend.

But that "reassuring" answer is actually frightening. Lawrence Summers calls today's arrangement "the balance of financial terror," and says that it is flawed in the same way that the "mutually assured destruction" of the Cold War era was. That doctrine held that neither the United States nor the Soviet Union would dare use its nuclear weapons against the other, since it would be destroyed in return. With allowances for hyperbole, something similar applies to the dollar stand-off. China can't afford to stop feeding dollars to Americans, because China's own dollar holdings would be devastated if it did. As long as that logic holds, the system works. As soon as it doesn't, we have a big problem.

China's lopsided growth—ahead in exports, behind in schooling, the environment, and everything else—makes the country socially less stable as it grows richer.

What might poke a giant hole in that logic? Not necessarily a titanic struggle over the future of Taiwan. A simple mistake, for one thing. Another speech by Cheng Siwei—perhaps in response to a provocation by [American CNN journalist] Lou Dobbs. A rumor that the oil economies are moving out of dollars for good, setting their prices in euros. Leaked suggestions that the Chinese government is hoping to buy Intel, leading to angry denunciations on the Capitol floor, leading to news that the Chinese will sit out the next Treasury auction. As many world tragedies have been caused by miscalculation as by malice.

Or pent-up political tensions, on all sides. China's lopsided growth—ahead in exports, behind in schooling, the environment, and everything else—makes the country socially less stable as it grows richer. Meanwhile, its expansion disrupts industries and provokes tensions in the rest of the world. The billions of dollars China pumps into the United States each week strangely seem to make it harder rather than easier for Americans to face their own structural problems. One day, something snaps. Suppose . . . [China makes a bad bet on a stock] . . . with billions of dollars of Chinese people's assets irretrievably wiped out. They will need someone to blame, and Americans, for their part, are already primed to blame China back.

So, the shock comes. Does it inevitably cause a cataclysm? No one can know until it's too late. The important question to ask about the U.S.-China relationship, the economist Eswar Prasad, of Cornell [University], recently wrote in a paper about financial imbalances, is whether it has "enough flexibility to withstand and recover from large shocks, either internal or external." He suggested that the contained tensions were so great that the answer could be no.

Today's American system values upheaval; it's been a while since we've seen too much of it. But Americans who lived through the Depression knew the pain real disruption can bring. Today's Chinese, looking back on their country's last century, know, too. With a lack of tragic imagination, Americans have drifted into an arrangement that is comfortable while it lasts, and could last for a while more. But not much longer.

Years ago, the Chinese might have averted today's pressures by choosing a slower and more balanced approach to growth. If they had it to do over again, I suspect they would in fact choose just the same path—they have gained so much, including the assets they can use to do what they have left undone, whenever the government chooses to spend them. The same is not true, I suspect, for the United States, which might have chosen a very different path: less reliance on China's subsidies, more reliance on paying as we go. But it's a little late for those thoughts now. What's left is to prepare for what we find at the end of the path we have taken.

CHAPTER 2

Who Oversees the Quality and Safety of Chinese Imports?

Chapter Overview

Murray M. Lumpkin

Murray M. Lumpkin is the deputy commissioner of international and special programs at the U.S. Department of Health and Human Services.

China is presently one of the world's largest producers and consumers of agricultural products, and [it] hopes to further increase agricultural production through improved plant stocks, fertilizers, and technology. China is now a major supplier to the U.S. of seafood, canned vegetables, fruit juices, honey, and numerous other varieties of processed foods. During the 1980's through the late 1990's, FDA [U.S. Food and Drug Administration] encountered several serious compliance problems with Chinese food exports, including lead and cadmium in ceramicware used to store and ship food products, and staphylococcal contamination of canned mushrooms.

While improvements have been made in some Chinese products with which we have had concerns in the past, there is unfortunately still a pattern of substandard products that continue to be shipped to the U.S. As all of you are very well aware, this pattern has continued, and the safety of food and other FDA-regulated products from China have become a concern for FDA, Congress, and U.S. consumers.

The Chinese food industry consists of large multi-national corporations, mid-size corporations and many small family-run operations. One of the challenges with the Chinese food industry is its sheer size and the number of people involved in the production and distribution chains. A good example of this challenge is evident in Chinese fishery and aquaculture production.

Murray M. Lumpkin, "Statement by Murray M. Lumpkin, M.D., Deputy Commissioner, International and Special Programs on Safety of Chinese Imports: Oversight and Analysis of the Federal Response, before Committee on Commerce, Science, and Transportation, U.S. Senate," www.hhs.gov/asl/testify/2007/07/t20070718a.html. July 18, 2007. Reproduced by permission.

Aquaculture Concerns

Commercialization and consumption of aquacultured (or farm-raised) seafood products has increased worldwide. Aquacultured seafood has become one of the fastest growing sectors of the world food economy, accounting for approximately half of all seafood production worldwide. Approximately 80 percent of the seafood consumed in the U.S. is imported from approximately 130 countries, including China. Over 40 percent of that seafood comes from aquaculture operations.

In terms of sheer volume, China is the largest exporter of seafood to the U.S.

China is the largest producer of aquacultured seafood in the world, accounting for approximately 70 percent of the total production and approximately 51 percent of the total value of aquacultured seafood exported around the world. In terms of monetary value, China is currently the second largest exporter of seafood to the U.S. including exports of shrimp and catfish. In terms of sheer volume, China is the largest exporter of seafood to the U.S. Shrimp and catfish products represent two of the top ten most consumed seafood products in the U.S. FDA and the National Oceanic and Atmospheric Administration work cooperatively regarding seafood safety risk assessment, management, and seafood safety research and monitoring.

As the aquaculture industry continues to grow in developing economies, concerns regarding the use of unapproved animal drugs and unsafe chemicals in aquaculture operations have increased substantially. The use of unapproved antibiotics or chemicals in aquaculture raises significant public health concerns. There is clear scientific evidence that the use of antibiotics, and other drugs and chemicals, such as malachite green, nitrofurans, fluoroquinolones, and gentian violet, during the various stages of aquaculture can result in the presence of residues of the parent compound or its metabolites that are found in the edible portion of the aquacultured seafood and can be potentially harmful to human health. Also, the use in aquaculture of unapproved antibiotics may significantly increase antimicrobial resistance to those antibiotics in human pathogens of public health concern.

Fluoroquinolones have been prohibited from extra-label use in the U.S. and many other parts of the world in aquaculture because of public health concern about the development of such antimicrobial resistance. Moreover, prolonged exposure to nitrofurans, malachite green, and gentian violet, or metabolites to these chemicals, has been shown to induce cancer in humans or animals.

From a legal and regulatory perspective, in the U.S., use of malachite green, nitrofurans, fluoroquinolones, or gentian violet as drugs in food-producing animals would require an approved new animal drug application under section 512 of the Federal Food, Drug, and Cosmetic (FD&C) Act. FDA has not approved these substances for use as drugs in aquacultured animals. . . .

FDA's Efforts to Protect Americans

FDA has been actively working to protect Americans from unsafe Chinese aquacultured seafood. For many years, FDA has been testing imports and has been working with counterpart agencies in other countries that also have been testing Chinese aquacultured seafood that is being offered for import into their countries. Using data from these testing programs, FDA has been placing companies whose products have been found to be violative on an import alert, whereby future shipments of the products can be refused admission into the U.S. until they are demonstrated to FDA to be free of these residues. In addition, FDA scientists have been working with their Chinese counterparts for several years in an effort to help them better understand our standards and the science that supports those standards. FDA colleagues have made trips to China to inspect specific aquaculture facilities and have conducted seminars and workshops in China to try to raise awareness among producers of the safety expectations of FDA regarding aquacultured seafood that they wish to ship to the U.S.

In February 2006, the [United States] became aware of a problem concerning contamination of honey with fluoroquinolones [a type of antibiotic].

In addition, the senior leadership of FDA and the senior leadership from its counterpart agencies in China (the State Food and Drug Administration [SFDA] and the General Administration for Quality Supervision, Inspection, and Quarantine) have had annual formal bilateral meetings since 2006 at which issues of special concern along with general topics regarding scientific approaches to product safety and quality are discussed. . . .

[In addition,] FDA and others within the [U.S.] Department of Health and Human Services are actively engaged with our Chinese counterparts in negotiating a comprehensive Memorandum of Understanding (MOU) that will include actions in many areas of food and feed production that should increase Americans' confidence in the safety of these Chinese products that are exported to the U.S. . . . Part of this MOU will be based on the positive outcomes experienced with two product-specific understandings that FDA and its Chinese counterparts have had in place for many years: an MOU covering ceramicware in which food is stored, and an arrangement with China regarding canned mushrooms that helps assure the safety of those products. These specific understandings have resulted in a marked decrease in health concerns related to these two Chinese products. The intent of the comprehensive MOU being negotiated at present is to achieve the same results not on a specific product basis, but on a national basis when it comes to FDA-regulated products being exported from China to the U.S.

[In March 2007, the] FDA found contaminants in wheat gluten imported into the U.S. from China and used as ingredients in pet food.

Honey Contamination

In February 2006, the Florida Department of Agriculture and Consumer Services became aware of a problem concerning contamination of honey with fluoroquinolones. They collected and analyzed samples of honey for residues of two of the fluoroquinolones of concern, ciprofloxacin and enrofloxacin. The State reported that residues of these antibiotics were found in honey that was traced back to a firm from China. Subsequently, on August 14, 2006, FDA issued Import Alert No. 36-04 requiring detention without physical examination of honey due to presence of fluoroquinolones. . . . [In March 2007, FDA updated] Import Alert No. 36-03 requiring detention without physical examination of honey due to presence of the antibiotic chloramphenicol. Fluoroquinolone antibiotics, including ciprofloxacin and enrofloxacin, have been used in the treatment of diseases in humans and animals. Enrofloxacin is approved for use in cattle but there are no other approvals for use in other food animals. The use of fluoroquinolones in honey bees or their environment can result in residues in honey. Fluoroquinolones are neither generally recognized as safe and effective to treat any honey bee diseases nor are they approved for such use. The use in apiculture (beekeeping) of unapproved antibiotics may significantly increase resistance to those antibiotics in human pathogens of public health concern. Fluoroquinolones have been prohibited from extra-label use in the U.S. in food producing animals because of concerns about the development of increased resistance and the resultant threat to public health. Use of fluoroquinolones to treat any honey bee disease is considered to be an unapproved new animal drug use within the meaning of section 512 of the FD&C Act.

Because of concerns about the presence of fluoroquinolones in the food supply, the U.S. is continuing to develop methods and strategies to detect illegal residues and prevent their introduction into the U.S. food supply.

Feed and Pet Food Ingredient Safety

On March 15, 2007, FDA learned that certain pet foods were sickening and killing cats and dogs. FDA found contaminants in wheat gluten imported into the U.S. from China and used as ingredients in pet food. Analysis by FDA's Forensic Chemistry Center revealed melamine and melamine analogues in the pet foods and in the wheat products used as an ingredient. FDA traced the suspect product to a single supplier in China, Xuzhou Anying Biologic Technology. FDA issued an import alert focused on this supplier, and began sampling 100 percent of all wheat gluten from China.

Melamine is a molecule that has a number of industrial uses, including use in manufacturing cooking utensils. It has not been approved for use as an ingredient in human or animal food in the U.S., and it is not permitted to be used as fertilizer in the U.S., as it is in some parts of the world.

Further investigation revealed that a portion of the melamine-tainted pet food was used to supplement swine and poultry feed on a small number of farms. FDA and the U.S. Department of Agriculture discovered that some animals that ate the tainted feed had been processed into human food. FDA subsequently learned that some of the contaminated wheat gluten was used to make fish feed. Due to the small amounts present and the small amounts that would be consumed in an average U.S. diet, government scientists have determined that there is no significant risk to human health from consuming food from animals that ate tainted feed. FDA and USDA [United States Department of Agriculture] continue their comprehensive investigation of this event.

Problems with Drugs Made in China

Chemical counterfeiting generally and diethylene glycol (DEG)-contaminated products specifically coming from China have been, and still are, on-going concerns for the U.S. and other nations. Ten years ago, Chinese counterfeit glycerin killed nearly 100 children in Haiti. Last year in Panama, Chinese glycerin contaminated with DEG again caused scores of deaths. Recently, toothpaste imported from China to the U.S. was found to contain DEG. It is our understanding that China does not require registration of chemicals that may have a dual use in both industrial chemical products and drug products. This is the case for dual-use chemicals targeted for domestic use as well as for export. With respect to dual-use chemicals, this systemic problem increasingly can pose a hazard to the U.S. drug supply if these products are exported as "chemicals" but used as starting products for the production of pharmaceuticals.

The recent DEG episode has reinvigorated attention on China's regulation of its drug products, active pharmaceutical ingredients, and excipients. FDA's general experience has been that, while some Chinese companies are state-of-the-art in technology and manufacturing expertise, many are at the opposite end of the spectrum. Further, [from 2003 to 2007], the number of FDA-registered drug manufacturers in China has at least doubled. . . .

Ensuring the safety of FDA-regulated products imported from China is a significant task, but . . . FDA is diligently working to efficiently and effectively use the resources and authorities we have been provided by Congress to help protect the public health of the U.S. and to help to provide safe products to U.S. consumers.

American and Chinese Supervision Is Crucial to Ensure Quality of Chinese Products

David J. Lynch

David J. Lynch is a reporter for USA Today, *a national U.S. newspaper.*

Killer pet food. Tainted toothpaste. Tires lacking an essential safety component. And now, seafood laced with potentially unhealthy levels of antibiotics.

Suddenly, "Made in China" looks like another way of saying: "Buyer beware."

Problems with Quality

In recent years, American consumers eagerly snapped up an ever-widening array of Chinese-made products, from Wal-Mart T-shirts and Dell laptops to Black & Decker power drills and Ethan Allen cabinets. It's no secret why multinational companies increased their reliance on Chinese factories: lower production costs. The recent spate of suspect Chinese imports, however, is raising troubling questions about the trade-offs involved in the relentless pursuit of rock-bottom prices.

Weak supervision by both the Chinese and U.S. governments is responsible for allowing subpar goods onto American store shelves.

"Sometimes, it's a shock to discover how poor the quality processes are," says Sebastien Breteau, chief executive of Asia

Inspection, a Hong Kong company that audits Chinese factories for 158 U.S. companies. "It's very, very common that the goods you receive are not exactly what you ordered, either because the factory can't deliver or because the definition of the product is not clear enough."

Breteau should know. In the mid-1990s, he started a small trading company in Hong Kong, specializing in inexpensive gifts manufactured in southern China. When word got out that he was personally inspecting his suppliers, other traders asked him to do the same for them.

Now, he has almost 1,000 clients from 58 countries. His inspectors performed about 25,000 one-day factory checks last year, with 23% of the facilities earning failing grades because of poor factory hygiene, inaccurate product manuals, cosmetic blemishes on finished goods, even installation of the wrong electrical plug.

Breteau's clients sometimes overlook minor shortcomings, but they still ultimately reject one of every 12 shipments. He blames unsatisfactory production on Western companies' ceaseless pressure for lower prices from Chinese suppliers. "It's not that they're dishonest. It's that they don't (always) have the technical level to produce to Western quality standards," he says.

Close Oversight Is in Question

Weak supervision by both the Chinese and U.S. governments is responsible for allowing subpar goods onto American store shelves, says Sen. Charles Schumer, D-N.Y., who called [in 2007] for creation of a new Commerce Department "import czar" to boost regulatory defenses.

The sudden U.S. focus on flawed Chinese goods threatens to exacerbate already tense Sino [Chinese]-U.S. trade relations. Much is at stake in the furor about Brand China: the low prices that consumers crave, multinationals' border-spanning supply chains and China's ability to produce enough jobs to preserve social stability.

"There's a cost, a huge cost, involved if the companies or the government do not handle this well. This is a very new concept for them [Chinese bussinesses]—post-sales service, product liability, the notion of a recall—because they are new-comers in the global economy," says Ming-jer Chen, a business professor at the University of Virginia.

U.S. companies, which operate their own factories in China and use Chinese suppliers, say they employ rigorous safe-guards to ensure that their goods are sound. Goodyear Tire & Rubber, for example, puts potential suppliers through an in-tense "process audit" of its production system and quality controls before placing its first order, Goodyear spokesman Ed Markey says. Goodyear suppliers also must obtain a certifica-tion called "ISO 9000," which attests to a company's use of consistent quality procedures and must be periodically re-newed.

The tiremaker has a corporate office in Shanghai, which allows it to maintain close oversight of a Chinese tire factory in nearby Hangzhou. That supplier began producing tires for Goodyear in the middle of [2006], for sale in the USA under private-label brands, not the Goodyear name, Markey says.

Each tire that comes off the Chinese assembly line is indi-vidually balanced and visually inspected. "If it doesn't meet the (Goodyear) standards, it's destroyed," Markey says.

Amid the recent cascade of Chinese import horror stories, some companies aren't eager to talk about their China links. In response to questions about their quality assurance pro-grams in China, Black & Decker, Dell, Wal-Mart and Ford Motor each provided general assurances of their commitment to quality but scant details on how it's achieved.

Black & Decker, for example, makes many of its power tools and locks in a factory it owns in Suzhou, outside Shanghai, and a separate 50/50 joint venture plant in Shenzhen, southern China's manufacturing boomtown. The company won't disclose whether it has accelerated planned plant inspections or made any other changes in response to recent events, says Mark Rothleitner, a company vice president.

In recent years, the company, which has additional Chinese facilities in Xiamen and Qingdao, has increased the share of its total output produced in China, Mexico and the Czech Republic, according to Securities and Exchange Commission filings. "We do have a very rigorous process for qualifying suppliers all over the globe. . . . The quality coming out of China is very good," Rothleitner says.

Ford Motor, which said [in 2006] it planned to buy up to $3 billion worth of auto parts from Chinese suppliers, didn't respond to a specific question about whether it was rethinking that plan. But in an e-mail exchange, spokesman Kenneth Hsu in Beijing wrote: "All the commodities purchased are tested against global specifications, regardless of where they are coming from."

No one's going to abandon a market of 1.3 billion people because of a few manufacturing stumbles.

Wal-Mart spokesman Kevin Gardner e-mailed a statement saying that "customer safety is a top priority" for the discount retailer, which spends more than $18 billion annually on products made in China. "Product samples are tested systematically before and during production by third-party testing labs, and our own quality-control staff conducts product inspections, as well," the statement said.

Telephone and e-mail requests for additional details, including the frequency of inspections, were not answered.

Considering Alternatives

No one's going to abandon a market of 1.3 billion people because of a few manufacturing stumbles. But some companies, already antsy about rising wages in southern China's export heartland, are undoubtedly rethinking their short-term sourcing plans, says David Powell, a partner in A.T. Kearney's Chicago office.

One of his clients—a *Fortune* 50 [listed in the top 50 companies by *Fortune* magazine] consumer-products company with its own factories in China, plus Chinese suppliers—is considering a shift of some production to nearby countries, Powell says. Fast-growing upstarts such as Vietnam now resemble the China of the 1990s, with their ample low-cost labor boasting adequate skills and a fierce work ethic.

The controversy about Chinese quality practices comes as imports from China are soaring. In 2006, the USA imported $288 billion worth of Chinese products—more than double the 2002 figure and more than 10 times the 1992 amount. Among the largest categories [in 2006] were: apparel, $25.6 billion; toys, $22.2 billion; televisions and VCRs, $14.5 billion; and furniture, $13.2 billion.

The USA also imported $28.9 billion worth of computer peripherals and $17.4 billion in computers. But about two-thirds of the value of the high-tech gear that the U.S. government records in its trade accounts as "Chinese" represents products assembled in Chinese factories using parts from other countries, says economist Nicholas Lardy of the Peterson Institute for International Economics.

A quarter century after it began embracing market-oriented reforms, China's exports remain concentrated in comparatively unsophisticated products. To date, the Chinese government's efforts to cultivate national champions in higher-end industries such as autos, aircraft and semiconductors have met with mixed results. [Chinese producer] Haier has carved out a profitable niche in the USA selling small refrigerators and other appliances. But Chinese automakers have penetrated only less competitive markets such as the Middle East.

A June 28 [2007] post on the *Autoblog.com* website gave a thumbs down to Brilliance China Automotive's hopes of selling its BS6 sedan in Europe following the car's woeful performance in a crash test.

The website published a photo of the Brilliance test vehicle crumpled like a beer can and this blunt appraisal: "Buyers get what they pay for. The BS6, as currently constructed, appears to be a complete piece of crap. The horrifying 40-mph offset frontal crash test video shows damage that can be described as catastrophic, at best."

Brilliance told Reuters that its European distributor still hopes to sell the car, despite it receiving just one out of five stars on the test, conducted by Germany's ADAC [Allgemeiner Deutscher Automobil Club, Europe's largest] auto club.

The Chinese government has an enormous stake in protecting the "Made in China" brand.

China Is Still Developing

It would be easy to mock Chinese aspirations to climb the value ladder. But Americans of a certain age recall in the 1960s similar doubts about the label "Made in Japan."

Considering the turmoil that enveloped China for most of the 20th century, the mystery isn't why Chinese factories are having some quality problems. The wonder is that they don't have far more. Consider that in 1986, Chinese exports to the USA totaled $4.7 billion. Today, Chinese factories ship more than that to American customers every week.

China is in the midst of an enormous transformation from an isolated, centrally planned, mostly rural nation into a fiercely competitive economic dynamo. Since joining the World Trade Organization in 2001, the country has overhauled thousands of laws and regulations to bring itself into conformance with the global economy's dictates.

But its effervescent economic growth—an annual rate of 10% since 1990—has outstripped the government's policing ability. Now, as questions mount about the safety and quality of its factories' output, China is under pressure to respond.

The Chinese government has an enormous stake in protecting the "Made in China" brand. Creating the millions of jobs required each year for new college graduates and farmers abandoning their fields for a better life in the cities demands strong export sales.

Even as they struggle to repair China's smudged image, Chinese officials see political overtones in the sudden surge of U.S. complaints about product quality and safety. [In 2007,] the Chinese embassy in Washington distributed a three-page statement defending the country's food exports and suggesting the issue was being exaggerated. "Certain isolated cases," the government document said, "should not be blown out of proportion to mislead the public into thinking that all food from China is unsafe."

China Has Taken Action Against Substandard Products

Consulate General of The People's Republic of China in Chicago

The Consulate General of The People's Republic of China in Chicago is an office maintained by China in the United States to promote cooperation and exchanges between the two countries, protect the legal rights of Chinese citizens in America, and provide consular services related to passport, visa, notary public, and authentification to both local Chinese and non-Chinese people.

China's quality supervision authorities have blacklisted 14 companies for planning to export substandard food products and banned them from further exports.

The companies were exposed by the General Administration of Quality Supervision, Inspection and Quarantine (GAQSIQ) on its official website, *www.aqsiq.gov.*

"They will be banned from exporting food products," Lin Wei, an official with the administration, said. . . .

The substandard products, which included preserved seafood and fruit, were destined to be exported to Japan, Canada, the United States and the European Union, according to the administration. Some of the products were found to contain additives such as sulphur dioxide in excess of levels set by the importing countries, or were found to be contaminated by harmful bacteria.

China's Inspection System

A total of 34,400 cases of fake and low-quality food have been cracked by China's industrial and commercial authorities in

Consulate General of The People's Republic of China in Chicago, "China Names and Shames Companies for Exporting Substandard Food Products," China Consulate Chicago, July 13, 2007. www.chinaconsulatechicago.org/eng/xw/t340087.htm. Copyright © 2007 Consulate General of The People's Republic of China in Chicago. Reproduced by permission.

the first half of [2007], involving goods worth 67.7 million yuan [Chinese dollar] (8.9 million U.S. dollars).

Sun Wenxu, an official with the State Administration for Industry and Commerce (SAIC) said [in 2007] that 3,191 food manufacturers had been shut down during the first six months of the year.

Investigations showed [that] two companies had managed to evade quality checks by labeling products as exports that were not subject to quality inspection.

Industrial and commercial departments checked nearly 130,000 fairs and wholesale markets and withdrew 5,757 tons of substandard food from the market, Sun said.

Lin said the government had paid great attention to recent health scares caused by substandard food products and great efforts were being made to prevent similar incidents.

In May [2007], China's quality control watchdog confirmed two domestic companies had exported melamine-contaminated wheat gluten and rice protein blamed for the deaths of dogs and cats in the United States.

Investigations showed the two companies had managed to evade quality checks by labeling products as exports that were not subject to quality inspection. However, Lin said the violation was only an "isolated" case and 99 percent of China's exported food was up to standard.

Lin said the government had set up a rigorous quality supervision and inspection system for exported food, which covered all procedures, including planting, processing, distributing and exporting.

"Starting from planting and breeding to exporting, all procedures are under close supervision," said Lin, deputy general director of the bureau of safety of exported and imported food under the administration.

Lin said China was open to cooperation and exchanges with other countries on food safety. "We are fully confident that Chinese products are not only affordable and fine quality, but also healthy and safe," Lin said.

Concerns About Small Factories

The government has come under great pressure to improve food safety following a series of controversies caused by substandard food, ranging from drug-tainted fish to banned Sudan dye used to color egg yolks red.

A survey showed that about 20 percent of products made in China for domestic consumption failed to meet quality and safety standards in the first half of 2007. The survey, conducted by the GAQSIQ, covered 7,200 different products from 6,362 enterprises, with an emphasis on food, daily commodities and farming machinery and fertilizers.

The administration found that 93.1 percent of products made by large enterprises were up to standard—the figure was 84.2 percent for medium-sized enterprises and 72.9 percent for small enterprises.

To improve food safety, the [Chinese] government laid out a five-year plan to tighten the supervision of food and drug products.

Wu Jianping, director of the department of production supervision under the GAQSIQ, said China had about 448,000 food manufacturers, 79 percent of which were small factories with fewer than 10 employees.

"Food produced by small factories and workshops is one of our top concerns, and the small food workshops are the key targets in our food safety campaign," Wu said.

To improve food safety, the government laid out a five-year plan to tighten the supervision of food and drug products and promised to "significantly reduce the number of incidents caused by substandard food or drug products" by 2010.

"China will try to reduce the number of small food workshops by half by 2010 so as to effectively curb illegal activities involving shoddy food products," Wu said.

The quality watchdog dealt with 23,000 cases of fake brand and substandard food from December 2006 to May 2007 and 180 food manufacturers were shut down for making substandard food or using inedible materials in production.

The U.S. Government Is Taking More Responsibility for Consumer Safety

Peter Grier

Peter Grier is a staff writer for The Christian Science Monitor, *a daily international newspaper published by the First Church of Christ, Scientist in Boston, Massachusetts.*

Lead in toys. Melamine in pet food. Toxic chemicals in toothpaste. And now, tainted pharmaceuticals.

The unfolding scandal of contaminated blood thinner from China is the latest in a string of revelations about dangerous imports from a country that has risen to become manufacturer to the world.

The Call for More Consumer Protection

US lawmakers now are pushing for more protection for American consumers, as hearings in Congress ... have made clear. Even the head of the [U.S.] Food and Drug Administration (FDA) says he needs more money—and a new approach—to try and ensure that products entering the country are safe.

In a world of increasingly globalized commerce, the next frontier may not be more or cheaper goods, but higher quality trade.

Other countries may well follow suit. In a world of increasingly globalized commerce, the next frontier may not be more or cheaper goods, but higher quality trade, says Moisés Naím, editor in chief of *Foreign Policy* magazine.

Peter Grier, "Tainted Chinese Imports Spur Calls to Protect Consumer," *The Christian Science Monitor*, April 24, 2008. www.csmonitor.com/2008/0424/p02s02-usgn.html. Reproduced by permission from Christian Science Monitor (www.csmonitor.com).

"What is now happening [with contaminated products] is going to create a big surge in consumer protection demands and expectations," says Mr. Naím, author of *Illicit*, a book that details some of the problems of globalization.

According to the FDA, as many as 81 Americans may have died after taking heparin, a blood thinning agent, tainted in China via the addition of a poisonous chemical. US recalls of Chinese heparin ingredients began in February [2008].

Chinese officials don't agree that the deaths were caused by contamination that may have occurred in their country. They say that the problem could stem from manufacturing of the finished drug at a plant in New Jersey.

More Money for the FDA

At a House [of Representatives] hearing [in April 2008] lawmakers chastised the FDA for not increasing its focus on foreign drug makers after the heparin crisis and other contamination scares.

The FDA inspects domestic drug plants every 2.7 years, on average, they noted. But at the rate they are moving, it would take 13 years to check every foreign drug plant and 1,900 years to check every foreign food plant that ships products to the US.

"It's clear the FDA needs some new thinking on how to deal with the 21st century," said Rep. Joe Barton [Republican] of Texas.

FDA commissioner Andrew von Eschenbach under questioning admitted that his agency needs more resources. The FDA would have to more than double its current $10 million budget for foreign inspections if it was to check every Chinese drug firm at the same rate it inspects US firms. But Dr. von Eschenbach added that he believes current inspections would not have caught the contaminated heparin because the toxic chemical it contained closely mimics genuine ingredients.

What's needed, he said, is a five-year improvement plan that adds new information systems and tests, and includes the opening of three planned FDA offices in China. "The solution needs to be much more comprehensive than just simply inspecting a facility," said the FDA chief. . . .

[The Senate] is set to address the same issues. The Senate has already passed a measure giving the FDA a 20 percent increase in funds, though it's unlikely the White House will give final approval to such a jump in appropriations.

Helping the Chinese

If the Chinese government inspection process was similar to that in the US, there would not be as much of a problem in regards to worry about tainted products entering America, says Joel Trachtman, a professor of international law at the Fletcher School at Tufts University in Medford, Mass. But it isn't. And right now "they don't coordinate very well," he says.

The main question for the US is not how to punish the Chinese, but how to assist them moving forward, he says. Chinese citizens do not want to suffer from tainted products anymore than citizens of other countries in the world. Nor does Beijing want to see exports wither due to foreign concerns. "China needs to understand its broader long-term commercial interests here," says Mr. Trachtman.

Right now, the FDA plans to open its Chinese offices in Beijing, Shanghai, and Guangzhou. They will employ 13 people—eight from the US, and five locals.

China has yet to agree to final implementation of this plan. But under the terms of the World Trade Organization—which both the US and China belong to—the US has every right to carry out intrusive inspections in China if there is a scientific basis for them, says Gary Hufbauer, a trade and regulation expert at the Peterson Institute for International Economics. "This has been quite damaging to China, but I think the authorities there realize this," says Mr. Hufbauer.

Overall, the demands of policing the vast quantity of products that flow across the world's borders are so large that they will require a global solution, Naím says.

Policymakers Are to Blame for Tainted Imports

Rick Weiss

Rick Weiss is a staff reporter for the Washington Post, *a prominent U.S. newspaper.*

D ried apples preserved with a cancer-causing chemical. Frozen catfish laden with banned antibiotics. Scallops and sardines coated with putrefying bacteria. Mushrooms laced with illegal pesticides.

These were among the 107 food imports from China that the [U.S.] Food and Drug Administration [FDA] detained at U.S. ports [in April 2007], agency documents reveal, along with more than 1,000 shipments of tainted Chinese dietary supplements, toxic Chinese cosmetics and counterfeit Chinese medicines.

Change will prove difficult ... because U.S. companies have become so dependent on the Chinese economy that tighter rules on imports stand to harm the U.S. economy, too.

Concerns About Chinese Food Imports

For years, U.S. inspection records show, China has flooded the United States with foods unfit for human consumption. And for years, FDA inspectors have simply returned to Chinese importers the small portion of those products they caught— many of which turned up at U.S. borders again, making a second or third attempt at entry.

Rick Weiss, "Tainted Chinese Imports Common: In Four Months, FDA Refused 298 Shipments," *The Washington Post*, May 20, 2007. www.washingtonpost.com/wp-dyn/content/article/2007/05/19/AR2007051901273.html. © 2007 The Washington Post Company. Reprinted with permission.

Now the confluence of two events—the highly publicized contamination of U.S. chicken, pork and fish with tainted Chinese pet food ingredients and [the 2007] resumption of high-level economic and trade talks with China—has activists and members of Congress demanding that the United States tell China it is fed up.

Dead pets and melamine-tainted food notwithstanding, change will prove difficult, policy experts say, in large part because U.S. companies have become so dependent on the Chinese economy that tighter rules on imports stand to harm the U.S. economy, too.

"So many U.S. companies are directly or indirectly involved in China now, the commercial interest of the United States these days has become to allow imports to come in as quickly and smoothly as possible," said Robert B. Cassidy, a former assistant U.S. trade representative for China and now director of international trade and services for Kelley Drye Collier Shannon, a Washington law firm.

As a result, the United States finds itself "kowtowing to China," Cassidy said, even as that country keeps sending American consumers adulterated and mislabeled foods.

It's not just about cheap imports, added Carol Tucker Foreman, a former assistant secretary of agriculture now at the Consumer Federation of America [an advocacy group]. "Our farmers and food processors have drooled for years to be able to sell their food to that massive market," Foreman said. "The Chinese counterfeit. They have a serious piracy problem. But we put up with it because we want to sell to them."

U.S. agricultural exports to China have grown to more than $5 billion a year—a fraction of [2006's] $232 billion U.S. trade deficit with China but a number that has enormous growth potential, given the Chinese economy's 10 percent growth rate and its billion-plus consumers.

Trading with the largely unregulated Chinese marketplace has its risks, of course, as evidenced by the many lawsuits that U.S. pet food companies now face from angry consumers who say their pets were poisoned by tainted Chinese ingredients. Until recently, however, many companies and even the federal government reckoned that, on average, those risks were worth taking. And for some products they have had little choice, as China has driven competitors out of business with its rock-bottom prices.

In the first four months of 2007, FDA inspectors—who are able to check out less than 1 percent of regulated imports—refused 298 food shipments from China.

But after the pet food scandal, some are recalculating.

"This isn't the first time we've had an incident from a Chinese supplier," said Pat Verduin, a senior vice president at the Grocery Manufacturers Association, a trade group in Washington [D.C.]. "Food safety is integral to brands and to companies. This is not an issue the industry is taking lightly."

New Focus on the Problem

China's less-than-stellar behavior as a food exporter is revealed in stomach-turning detail in FDA "refusal reports" filed by U.S. inspectors: Juices and fruits rejected as "filthy." Prunes tinted with chemical dyes not approved for human consumption. Frozen breaded shrimp preserved with nitrofuran, an antibacterial that can cause cancer. Swordfish rejected as "poisonous."

In the first four months of 2007, FDA inspectors—who are able to check out less than 1 percent of regulated imports—refused 298 food shipments from China. By contrast, 56 shipments from Canada were rejected, even though Canada exports about $10 billion in FDA-regulated food and agricultural products to the United States—compared to about $2 billion from China.

China is not certified to sell any meat to the United States because it has not met [U.S. food safety] requirement[s].

Although China is subject to more inspections because of its poor record, those figures mean that the rejection rate for foods imported from China, on a dollar-for-dollar basis, is more than 25 times that for Canada.

Miao Changxia, of the Chinese Embassy in Washington, said China "attaches great importance" to the pet food debacle. "Investigations were immediately carried out . . . and a host of emergency measures have been taken to ensure the hygiene and safety of exported plant-origin protein products," she said in an e-mail.

But deception by Chinese exporters is not limited to plant products, and some of their most egregiously unfit exports are smuggled into the United States.

Under Agriculture Department rules, countries cannot export meat and poultry products to the United States unless the USDA [U.S. Department of Agriculture] certifies that the slaughterhouses and processing plants have food-safety systems equivalent to those here. Much to its frustration, China is not certified to sell any meat to the United States because it has not met that requirement.

But that has not stopped Chinese meat exporters. In the past year, USDA teams have seized hundreds of thousands of pounds of prohibited poultry products from China and other Asian countries, Agriculture Secretary Mike Johanns announced in March [2007]. Some were shipped in crates labeled "dried lily flower," "prune slices" and "vegetables," according to news reports. It is unclear how much of the illegal meat slipped in undetected.

Chinese Chickens

Despite those violations, the Chinese government is on track to get permission to legally export its chickens to the United States—a prospect that has raised concern not only because of fears of bacteria such as salmonella but also because Chinese chickens, if not properly processed, could be a source of avian flu, which public-health authorities fear may be poised to trigger a human pandemic.

[In 2006], under high-level pressure from China, the USDA passed a rule allowing China to export to the United States chickens that were grown and slaughtered in North America and then processed in China—a rule that quickly passed through multiple levels of review and was approved the day before Chinese President Hu Jintao arrived in Washington last April [2006].

Now the rule that China really wants, allowing it to export its own birds to the United States, is in the works, said Richard Raymond, USDA's undersecretary for food safety. Reports in China have repeatedly hinted that only if China gets its way on chicken exports to the United States will Beijing lift its four-year-old ban on importing U.S. beef. Raymond denies any link.

"It's not being facilitated or accelerated through the system at all," Raymond said of the chicken rule, adding that permission for China to sell poultry to the United States is moving ahead because recent USDA audits found China's poultry slaughterhouses to be equivalent to those here.

It is not just that food from China is cheap. . . . For a growing number of important food products, China has become virtually the only source in the world.

Tony Corbo, a lobbyist for Food and Water Watch, a Washington advocacy group, said that finding—which is not subject to outside review—is unbelievable, given repeated findings of unsanitary conditions at China's chicken slaughter-houses. Corbo said he has seen some of those audits. "Everyone who has seen them was grossed out," he said.

An Official Response

The Cabinet-level "strategic economic dialogue" with China, which began in September [2006] . . . , was described early on as a chance for the United States and China to break a long-standing stalemate on trade issues. When it comes to the safety of imported foods, though, they may highlight the limited leverage that the United States has.

It is not just that food from China is cheap, said William Hubbard, a former associate director of the FDA. For a growing number of important food products, China has become virtually the only source in the world. China controls 80 percent of the world's production of ascorbic acid, for example, a valuable preservative that is ubiquitous in processed and other foods. Only one producer remains in the United States, Hubbard said.

"That's true of a lot of ingredients," he said, including the wheat gluten that was initially thought to be the cause of the pet deaths. Virtually none of it is made in the United States, because the Chinese sell it for less than it would cost U.S. manufacturers to make it.

So pervasive is the U.S. hunger for cheap imports, experts said, that the executive branch itself has repeatedly rebuffed proposals by agency scientists to impose even modest new safety rules for foreign foods. "Sometimes guidances can get through, but not regulations," said Caroline Smith DeWaal, food safety director at the Center for Science and the Public Interest, an advocacy group. Guidances, which the FDA defines as "current thinking on a particular subject," are not binding. Under the Bush administration in particular, DeWaal said, if a proposed regulation does get past agency or department heads, it hits the wall at the White House Office of

Management and Budget [OMB] [the agency responsible for submitting an annual budget to Congress].

A growing number of [U.S.] companies and trade groups . . . are speaking in favor of at least a little more protection, starting with a doubling of the FDA's food safety budget.

Andrea Wuebker, an OMB spokeswoman, said that the office reviewed 600 proposed rules last year and that it is up to agencies to finalize rules after they are reviewed. She did not tally how many reviews sent agencies' rule-writers back to the drawing board. She noted that some food safety rules have been finalized, including some related to mad cow disease and bioterrorism. Critics point out that the bioterrorism-related regulations were required by an act of Congress.

John C. Bailar III, a University of Chicago professor emeritus who chaired a 2003 National Academies committee that recommended major changes in the U.S. food safety system—which have gone largely unheeded—said he has become increasingly concerned that corporations and the federal government seem willing to put the interests of business "above the public welfare."

"This nation has—and has had for decades—a pressing need for a wholly dedicated food safety agency, one that is independent and not concerned with other matters . . . to bring together and extend the bits of food safety activities now scattered over more than a dozen agencies," he said in an e-mail.

Legislation to create such an agency was recently introduced, though many suspect that is too big a challenge politically.

But in the aftermath of the recent food scandals, a growing number of companies and trade groups, including Grocery Manufacturers of America, are speaking in favor of at least a little more protection, starting with a doubling of the FDA's food safety budget.

China is talking tough, too. "Violations of the rules on the use and addition of chemicals or other banned substances will be dealt with severely," said Miao, of the Chinese Embassy.

It is a threat some doubt will be enforced with great vigor, but nonetheless it reveals that China recognizes that the latest scandal has shortened Americans' fuses.

Chinese Producers Maintain Low Standards

WorldNetDaily

WorldNetDaily *is an independent news company dedicated to revitalizing the role of the free press in the United States.*

While China continues to promise to impose higher safety standards on exports, a WND [WorldNetDaily] study shows two of every three products recalled by the Consumer Product Safety Commission [CPSC] last year [2007] were Chinese imports—with an upward trend of defective, unsafe products found in every quarter of 2007.

Chinese Product Recalls

The CPSC recalled a total of 447 products for safety concerns last year [2007]. Of those, 298 were manufactured in China. Only 62 were made in the USA. The rest were made in other countries.

In 2006, the CPSC recalled a total of 467 kinds of products—221 of which were Chinese imports. Only 113 were for products made in the USA.

The trend illustrates not only vastly different standards in safety between the two countries, but also a massive shift in manufacturing from the U.S. to China.

As recently as 2002, the figures were virtually reversed—with 150 U.S. made products being recalled and just 99 from China.

The trend illustrates not only vastly different standards in safety between the two countries, but also a massive shift in manufacturing from the U.S. to China. The Chinese products recalled in 2007 include:

- Portable baby swings that entrap youngsters, resulting in 60 reports of cuts, bruises and abrasions;

- Swimming pool ladders that break, resulting in 127 reports of injuries, including leg lacerations requiring up to 21 stitches, five reports of bone fractures, two back injuries, two reports of torn ligaments and eight sprained ankles;

- Faulty baby carriers that result in babies falling out and getting bruised, getting skulls cracked and hospitalizations;

- Easy-Bake Ovens that trap children's fingers in openings, resulting in burns;

- Oscillating tower fans whose faulty wiring results in fires, burns and smoke inhalation injuries;

- Exploding air pumps that have resulted in 13 lacerations including six facial injuries and one to the eye;

- Bargain-priced oil-filled electric heaters, selling for less than $50, that burn down homes;

- Notebook computer batteries that burn up computers, cause other property damage and burn users;

- Circular saws with faulty blade guards that result in cutting users, not wood.

The Dangers Abound

Last year [2007] Chinese imports were hit for poisoning America's pets, risking America's human food supply and re-introducing lead poisoning to America's children. Electrical products made in China represent a significant percentage of the recalls. The CPSC noted the market is saturated with counterfeit circuit breakers, power strips, extension cords, batteries and holiday lights that are causing fires, explosions, shocks and electrocutions.

"Many counterfeit products are made in China and CPSC is actively working with the Chinese government to reduce the number of unsafe products that are exported to the United States," said the alert issued in May [2007]. The agency suggests that if the price of such an item seems to be too good to be true, it could be because the product is an inferior or unsafe counterfeit.

You might think an attractive, normal-looking table lamp would be safe. But 1,500 manufactured in China had to be recalled because of faulty light sockets that posed the risk of electrical shocks and fire hazards.

Or how about emergency lights that look just like other emergency lights but whose circuit board malfunctions, preventing illumination during emergencies? The CPSC recalled thousands of those in 2007.

And be careful which heated massaging recliners you relax in. If you choose one of the 1,700 manufactured in China and recalled by the commission last year, you might have found yourself medium rare because of an overheating and burn hazard discovered.

Even the simplest, most inexpensive items from China seem to pose massive risks. About 2,700 $12 pine cone candles had to be recalled when it was determined the exterior coating, not just the wick, caught fire.

Safety Issues

The problem is Americans see a cheap electrical power strip with a circuit breaker and assume it does what it is supposed to do. That is not the case with many Chinese counterfeits. They are not only counterfeits in the sense of improperly using brand names, they are actually counterfeits in the sense of pretending to do something they were never intended to do.

But big problems occur when an over-taxed power strip doesn't trip a circuit. Fires can occur. Property can be damaged. People can be killed.

Likewise, when Americans buy attractive-looking glassware at a bargain price, they might ask themselves: "How can I go wrong?"

Pier 1 Imports found out when 180,000 pieces of glassware were ordered recalled by the CPSC because the items broke for no apparent reason, sometimes cutting the hands of those holding them.

How could one go wrong purchasing an attractive kitchen stool engraved with a rooster on the seat? After all, it was only $30. Well, several people found out when the stools collapsed, even under the weight of small children.

A slew of Chinese [food] exports were banned or turned away by U.S. inspectors.

You might want to think twice before entrusting your child to something as simple as a crib made in China. For years, American manufacturers scrupulously lived up to the exacting safety standards imposed by agencies like the CPSC. Not so with Chinese manufacturers. Some 40,000 cribs had to be recalled when it was discovered directions instructed consumers to assemble them in ways that would result in the baby falling out and becoming entrapped. Additionally, locking pins on the side of the crib could pop off and cause a choking hazard.

About 450,000 infant car seat carriers manufactured in China had to be recalled when it was determined infants were falling out because of a faulty design. The Evenflo Co., which imported the carriers from China, received 679 reports of the handle on the car seat releasing for no reason, resulting in 160 injuries to children, including a skull fracture, two concussions and cuts and bruises.

American manufacturers also adapted years ago to requirements that products designed for young children avoid small parts that could result in choking accidents. But, again, based on a survey of recalls in the first six months of 2007, this seems to be a foreign concept among Chinese companies.

Even books for young children have been found to contain plastic squeaker toys that have become lodged in babies' throats and metal clips that break off, potentially injuring kids. Graco received 137 reports of infants mouthing, chewing and sometimes choking on tiny pieces of its soft blocks tower toys imported from China. At least 32 infants were found gagging on the pieces and 49 choked on the plastic covering. In all, 40,000 had to be recalled.

Food Products Also a Problem

It's not just the CPSC turning away Chinese imports. The Food and Drug Administration was busy in 2007 as well. A slew of Chinese exports were banned or turned away by U.S. inspectors, including wheat gluten tainted with the chemical melamine that has been blamed for dog and cat deaths in North America, monkfish that turned out to be toxic pufferfish, drug-laced frozen eel and juice made with unsafe color additives.

As WND reported last year, China, the leading exporter of seafood to the U.S., is raising most of its fish products in water contaminated with raw sewage and compensating by using dangerous drugs and chemicals, many of which are banned by the FDA.

The stunning news followed WND's report that FDA inspectors report tainted food imports from China are being rejected with increasing frequency because they are filthy, are contaminated with pesticides and tainted with carcinogens, bacteria and banned drugs.

China consistently has topped the list of countries whose products were refused by the FDA—and that list includes many countries, including Mexico and Canada, who export far more food products to the U.S. than China.

While less than half of Asia has access to sewage treatment plants, aquaculture—the raising of seafood products—has become big business on the continent, especially in China. In China, No. 1 in aquaculture in the world, 3.7 billion tons of sewage is discharged into rivers, lakes and coastal water— some of which are used by the industry. Only 45 percent of China has any sewage-treatment facilities, putting the country behind the rest of Asia.

Chinese Producers Are Exporting Increasingly Dangerous Products

Jim Ostroff

Jim Ostroff is the associate editor of The Kiplinger Letter, *a weekly newsletter published by the Kiplinger organization, a leader in personal finance and business forecasting.*

Steel imports from China that fall apart easily are making U.S. manufacturers and constructions firms more than a little nervous. Reports of failures during initial fabrication and questions about certification documents will mean closer scrutiny. The American and Canadian institutes of steel construction have already advised member companies to be vigilant and report any problems.

Worries for Structural Engineers

The biggest concern is hollow structural sections widely used in construction of skyscrapers, bridges, pipelines, office, commercial and school buildings. This high-strength steel is also commonly used in power lifts, cranes, farm equipment, furniture and car trailer hitches.

Chinese high-strength steel tubes and pipes are also a potential problem. They're used extensively in power plants and in large industrial boilers, and must withstand enormous pressures and hellish heat around the clock for weeks or months on end. This kind of steel also is used extensively in scaffolding that's erected on building exteriors during construction or renovation, as well as for interior work.

Inferior high-strength steel could cause catastrophic failures of buildings, pipelines or in power plants' boiler tubing.

Jim Ostroff, "New Threat from China: Shoddy Steel Imports," *Kiplinger Business Resource Center*, September 7, 2007. www.kiplinger.com/businessresource/forecast/archive /New_Threat_from_China_Steel_070907.html. All Contents © 2008 The Kiplinger Washington Editors. Reproduced by permission.

This is a large worry for structural engineers who will be working overtime as states embark on what amounts to a crash program to shore up bridges, following the collapse of the Minnesota span over the Mississippi River [in 2007]. China is already seeing problems. A Chinese power plant exploded recently when high-strength steel tubing blew out, says Roger Schagrin, general counsel for the Committee on Pipe and Tube Imports, which represents U.S. manufacturers of these products.

Dan Malone, construction manager for Garneau Manufacturing, based in Morinville, Alberta, Canada, an energy service company that works with many imports, said tests on a lot of 80 tons of Chinese steel tube products found "the welds failed horribly." Malone said there was no question that if the steel had been fabricated into a finished product and installed it would have failed and "would have killed somebody."

Imports of high-strength steel products from China are likely to plummet as result of [quality] concerns.

It's unlikely that existing buildings or bridges are in imminent danger of collapse. U.S. metals fabricators periodically test imported steels to assure they meet specs for strength, hardness and durability. Construction firms generally do likewise. It is possible that some of the substandard Chinese high-strength steel did slip through, so expect construction companies to recheck with their suppliers to determine whether any of the steel they used was purchased from Chinese mills. If so, U.S. contractors, building owners and power plant operators will bring in structural engineers to test the steel. If any structurally deficient steel is found, companies will shore up pillars, girders and trusses or replace boiler pipes entirely.

The End for Chinese Steel Imports?

Imports of specialized structural pipe and tubing steel from China are soaring, up from almost nothing two years ago to

102,000 metric tons in the first six months of this year [2007], according to American Iron and Steel Institute data. China now provides about 25% of U.S. supplies of this high-strength steel, making it the second-largest source behind Canada. U.S. steel mills supply about 16%.

U.S. and Canadian manufacturers and steel wholesaler service centers started testing hollow structural steel and other high-strength Chinese steels a few months ago when suspicions arose over mass-produced documents certifying that the tubular products met strength standards of the ASTM [American Society for Testing and Materials] International, a private group that sets standards for industrial and consumer goods. This reflects on the nature of Chinese companies hell-bent on jumping on the country's industrial boom bandwagon. "Most of China's 800-plus steelmakers are small fabricators who have no idea what quality is about, so there is a risk that some guy with a welding torch buys some hot-rolled coil steel and just welds it together," says Charles Bradford, president of Bradford Research, a metals consulting firm

Imports of high-strength steel products from China are likely to plummet as result of concerns. This will benefit Canadian suppliers and some U.S. steel specialty firms such as Atlas Tube, Columbia Structural Tubing, Ex-L-Tube, Ipsco, Longhorn Tube, Novamerican Steel and others.

Current
CONTROVERSIES

CHAPTER 3

Is the Trade Deficit with China a Threat to the U.S. Economy?

Chapter Preface

The United States and China have been trading partners since 1979, when the two countries first established normal trading relations. In 1979, the total value of U.S.-China trade was $2.4 billion, but it grew rapidly. By 2005 it reached $211.6 billion. Since then, trade volume between the two nations has accelerated even more, at an average rate of growth of 27.4 percent per year. Today, the United States is China's biggest trading partner and top export destination, and U.S. exports to China are rising at an annual rate of approximately 21.5 percent for the past several years. Total trade between China and the United States in 2007 was estimated by the U.S. government at $386.7 billion.

However, the U.S-China trade relationship is increasingly characterized by a significant imbalance, namely that the United States imports far more goods from China than it exports to the country. This imbalance is commonly referred to as the U.S.-China trade deficit. January 1985 was the last time that the United States exported more goods to China than it imported. Beginning in February 1985, Chinese imports to the United States began growing, and they have continued to do so each year since. In 2007, the trade deficit with China exceeded $256 billion, and today it grows by about $1 billion each day.

Many Americans, including some experts and policymakers, worry about this growing imbalance and believe it makes the United States too dependent upon China for our imports. The fact that China has used its trade surplus to invest heavily in U.S. treasury notes adds to the worry, because it means that China is now a major creditor of U.S. debt, giving it even more leverage over the United States and its economy.

However, not all economists agree with these concerns. Many commentators have pointed out that critics of the bilateral deficit often fail to consider that many of the imports are not made by Chinese companies, but instead are products manufactured in China by U.S. and other foreign multinational firms. Others say that China has simply replaced all the other Asian producers the United States used to import from. According to this view, U.S.-Chinese trade relations are healthy and have produced many positive effects for the United States, mainly cheap manufactured goods that have had the effect of keeping prices and inflation low for U.S. consumers.

Supporters of China trade basically believe that it makes sense for U.S. companies to ship manufacturing overseas, where labor costs are low, so that U.S.-based companies can focus on high-tech inventions and other high-value businesses that such developing economies as China's cannot duplicate. This, in essence, is the best argument in favor of global free-market-oriented trade—that it ultimately will free up each country to sell what it is best equipped to produce.

Despite these pro-China arguments, members of the U.S. Congress often have accused China of various unfair trade practices and pressured China to take actions to reduce the trade deficit. For example, U.S. senators have repeatedly urged China to allow its currency, the yuan (also known as the renminbi or RMB), to rise in value. Critics argue that China has kept the value of the yuan artificially low to suppress the prices of Chinese goods and encourage exports, thus adding to the trade deficit. In response to these pressures, China in July 2005 agreed to a 2.1 percent increase of the yuan's value and promised to allow its currency to float more freely in world markets. Since then the yuan has appreciated another 7 percent against the U.S. dollar, but critics argue that China has not delivered on its promise to let the market determine the yuan's value. Some economists, for example, believe the yuan remains undervalued by as much as 40 percent.

As the United States deals with rising inflation and a slowing U.S. economy, the issue of the trade deficit with China is likely to become even more of a political concern. The viewpoints in this chapter help to capture some of the competing arguments concerning whether or not the trade imbalance between the two countries constitutes a threat to the long-term health of the U.S. economy.

U.S.-China Trade Has Distorted the American Economy

Thomas I. Palley

Thomas I. Palley runs the Economics for Democratic and Open Societies Project, a program that seeks to stimulate public discussion about what kinds of economic conditions are needed to promote democracy and an open society. He also writes a weekly economic policy blog at www.thomaspalley.com.

For the last several years, China's undervalued exchange rate has been imposing large, costly distortions on the American economy. Unfortunately, the [George W.] Bush administration has taken no action.

Instead, it has allied itself with multinational corporations who are profiting handsomely from the current U.S.-China economic relationship, which allows them to earn huge margins on the cheap Chinese products they import. If the president won't take decisive action to get China to significantly revalue its exchange rate, Congress should. Here is an economic indictment against China that justifies such action.

Damages Caused by the Trade Deficit

The principal focus of attention has been the United States' trade deficit with China. Over the past four years the U.S.-China deficit grew from $83 billion in 2001 to $202 billion in 2005, and has been growing much faster than the U.S. deficit with the rest of the world. Moreover, China's impact is widely believed to extend beyond this direct effect. This is because many East Asian countries hold down their exchange rates for fear of losing competitiveness relative to China, thereby raising their trade surpluses with the United States.

The trade deficit has had several damaging effects. One of the most harmful is the destruction of manufacturing jobs, with many companies closing U.S. plants because they cannot compete. Some companies have simply gone out of business, while others have relocated or subcontracted production to China. Companies have redirected new investment to China rather than building new, modern capacity in the United States. This has structurally weakened the U.S. industrial base.

China's creation of artificially low interest rates has also contributed to America's housing price inflation.

The trade deficit also helps explain why this economic recovery has been the weakest since World War II. Instead of creating jobs at home, consumer spending has leeched out of the economy in the form of spending on imports. In the past, consumer spending would have created hundreds of thousands of domestic manufacturing jobs. This time 'round it created them in China.

Washington's free-trade lobby trumpets how consumers enjoy low prices. This is true. The sting that they have omitted is that consumers are also now loaded with debt and we have not created the jobs and investments that generate future income to repay those debts. This spells economic trouble down the road.

Another distortion concerns financial markets. For much of last year [2005] Federal Reserve officials wondered why long-term U.S. interest rates were not rising despite the Fed [Federal Reserve System, the central bank of the United States] raising short-term interest rates. The reason is that China (and other East Asian countries) has been buying U.S. bonds with its trade surplus. These purchases have held interest rates down and kept China's currency undervalued.

This distortion of financial markets has had serious consequences. In the past when the economy strengthened, long-term interest rates rose automatically and provided an automatic stabilizing mechanism. This time round that mechanism has been absent.

China's creation of artificially low interest rates has also contributed to America's housing price inflation. By keeping interest rates down, China has artificially kept mortgage rates down and thereby contributed to a possible U.S. housing price bubble. If there is a bubble, when it goes flat millions of households will find that they have over-paid for their homes and will be left holding large losses. These losses stand to be far larger than any conceivable consumer price savings from cheap Chinese products, and the debts incurred will also act as a drag on future economic activity and employment.

A related impact from China's distorting effect on financial markets concerns the pattern of investment. Lower interest rates are a positive factor for investment, but China's under-valued currency discourages investment in manufacturing. Consequently, the pattern of investment has been twisted, with under-investment in the traded goods sector (manufacturing) and possible over-investment in the non-traded sector (services and construction). This risks a repeat of the 1990s' "new economy," when much investment in start-up firms turned out to be wasteful.

Finally, China's under-valued currency has impacted the U.S. economy through China's impact on Mexico. For the past several years [before 2006] the business press has been full of stories of manufacturing firms leaving Mexico and going to China where wages and labor standards are even lower and the exchange rate is under-valued. The closure of Mexican factories and the loss of Mexican manufacturing jobs have in turn increased illegal immigration into the United States. This has increased the labor supply, and contributed to additional downward wage pressures at the low skill end of the labor market.

Problems for Other Developing Countries

In a global economy, economic dislocations within countries can have ramifications far beyond the countries directly involved. China's under-valued currency and unfair trading practices policies have been causing problems for the entire developing world by sucking jobs and foreign investment away from these countries. With regard to Mexico, these problems have imposed significant additional costs on the United States.

Free trade economists like to talk of China having what is called a "comparative advantage"—an argument for why it can be beneficial for two countries to trade—in manufacturing, and they use that talk to justify China's trade surplus. This talk is bogus. The theory of comparative advantage assumes that countries will have overall balanced trade. According to China's own statistical agency, China has a massive global trade surplus and last year's data showed it increased further. Additionally, there is robust evidence that China's official statistics are under-stated. This speaks to the distorted pattern of China's trade. China is not trading on the basis of comparative advantage, but on the basis of an artificially under-valued exchange rate and mercantilist commercial policies that subsidize exports and restrict imports.

In a market economy, distortions in one market spill over and cause distortions in other markets. The U.S. is a market economy, and China has distorted the pattern of international trade and U.S. financial markets. Exchange rates and interest rates are perhaps the two most important prices in the U.S. economy, and China has been distorting both. These distortions have generated huge costly misallocations of resources within the U.S. economy that will have lasting consequences, and China's policies have also injured developing countries.

Case closed!

The U.S.-China Trade Deficit Could Cause Economic Disaster for the United States

Jack Davis

Jack Davis is the founder and owner of I Squared R Element Co., the largest U.S. manufacturer of heating elements. He has more than fifty years of experience in manufacturing and foreign commerce.

Asian leaders who dupe our leaders and take advantage of our free trade policies with their predatory trade policies are draining the United States of its economic wealth. The communist Chinese leaders take offense to our superpower status and show hostility to our naval fleet in oceans bordering their shores.

China does not have to fight a war to have the fleet go home. It is much easier and less costly to mislead and deceive our government officials into making decisions that destroy our wealth-producing manufacturing capacity. Cheap labor, the visions of large markets and the greed for profits have seduced our transnational corporate owners. They outsource labor, capital, technology, research and development, manufacturing know-how and trade secrets. They are dismantling our wealth-producing industries. These owners and managers have no loyalty or allegiance to the United States. As our economic strength declines, so will our Navy's presence in the Pacific and our ability to defend our country.

Economic Damage to the United States

The Chinese already have accomplished so much economic damage, it is dangerous and frightening.

Jack Davis, "U.S. Must Prepare for Day of Reckoning," *Buffalo News*, January 13, 2008. http://jackdavis.org/news/writings/20080113_buffalonews/. Reproduced by author's permission.

We had a total trade deficit of $764 billion in 2006—a new record. With China, the trade deficit was $233 billion—the largest ever with a single country. [From 2003 to 2008], the U.S. trade deficit with China has increased by 20 percent each year.

Trade is necessary for America to prosper, but it must be balanced trade. Our total national debt is $9 trillion. About $5 trillion is owed to foreign countries and $1.3 trillion of that to China. All three numbers are pointing to economic crises.

The United States is living beyond its means—borrowing $2 billion a day from foreign countries to maintain our standard of living. A nation with a large trade deficit is similar to a person living above his means. If you have a successful career but lose your source of income, you still may have credit available on credit cards and ownership in your home and car. Thus, you can continue to maintain your standard of living for a while by increasing debt on your credit card or refinancing or selling your home and car.

Many Americans fail to see the . . . damage caused by the predatory trade policies that result in huge trade deficits and a huge national debt.

But just as a person cannot continually increase debt, neither can a nation. The key difference between a nation and a person is that a nation can print money and delay the day of reckoning. Eventually, foreign countries will not accept pieces of paper with pictures of our past presidents on them of decreasing value for their products or in payment of debt.

The U.S. dollar . . . has lost 50 percent of its value [from 2001–2008] in relation to the euro and will continue to decline in value. At some point, the U.S. dollar as the world's reserve currency will be replaced.

In addition to the $5 trillion we owe foreign countries, they also own or control more than 8,000 U.S. companies with a value of $8 trillion. Many of these companies were bought with the intent of gaining global control of key technologies and raw materials needed to produce advanced weapons, such as airplanes, computers, satellites and intercontinental ballistic missiles.

The United States Is Blind to the Coming Economic Crisis

When blindly following the ideology of free trade, many Americans fail to see the connection and damage caused by the predatory trade policies that result in huge trade deficits and a huge national debt—a portion of which is owed to foreign countries. Most Americans believe we are a superpower. It is only our military that is a superpower. Our economy is second- or third-world class. Most Americans don't see or understand the emerging economic disaster.

Our government officials continue to encourage companies to offshore research and development, engineering and manufacturing.

The Wall Street Journal reported on Dec. 20, [2007] that the U.S. Treasury Department once again declined to designate China as a currency manipulator. All of the numbers indicate the yuan [Chinese dollar] is 20 percent to 50 percent lower than its true market value when compared to the U.S. dollar. This is no accident. The Chinese are currency manipulators. This provides exports from China with large price advantages when competing with U.S. companies. This causes many U.S. companies to fail or be so weakened they permit foreign companies to buy them at a large discount.

China also promotes exports and discourages imports. It keeps wages low, rebates value-added taxes on its exports and charges value-added taxes on imports. It counterfeits and steals copyrights, trademarks and patents. It provides domestic industries with local tax incentives, offers special financing and charges tariffs on imports. It targets specific industries to monopolize.

No U.S. company can compete with these predatory practices. All of the above violate the World Trade Organization [WTO] regulations. Even with what appears to be numerous violations, the U.S. Treasury and Commerce departments fail to take action against China.

American politicians made a terrible mistake in 1996 when they voted to join the WTO. They gave Third World country bureaucrats control of U.S. international commerce. It is very difficult for the United States to win a case at the WTO. Most foreign Third World country bureaucrats dislike the United States. Also, many are as corruptible as the bureaucrats at the United Nations have proven to be. The chances of the U.S. getting fair treatment at the WTO are remote.

The U.S. Constitution states: "Congress shall have the power to regulate commerce with foreign nations." But Congress gave control of foreign commerce to the WTO. Congress must do what the people elected its members to do, and what they were sworn to do—"regulate commerce with foreign nations." Congress must immediately cancel U.S. membership in the WTO. If it doesn't, Asian countries will continue their predatory trade practices, continue destroying or buying U.S. companies, continue financing our debt, and continue buying our country. They will do this until we have nothing left to sell—no industries, no real estate and no natural resources.

The U.S. government will then have additional trillions of dollars of debt. If a government could be bankrupt, it would be. Social Security, Medicare and pensions will be without funds. All of our wealth-producing industries, mines and farms will be foreign-owned. The government's ability to tax will be significantly reduced along with its ability to defend our country.

The career politicians we sent to Washington still don't see or understand the coming economic crisis. None of the leading presidential candidates from either party seems to be aware of the coming economic crisis.

Wake up America, our day of reckoning is coming.

The Economic Threat from China Is Real

Paul Craig Roberts

Paul Craig Roberts is a writer who formerly held positions as assistant secretary of the U.S. Treasury during Ronald Reagan's presidency, associate editor of The Wall Street Journal, *and contributing editor of* National Review.

Twenty-four hours after I reported China's announcement that China, not the Federal Reserve [the central bank of the U.S. government], controls US interest rates by its decision to purchase, hold, or dump US Treasury bonds, the news of the announcement appeared in sanitized and unthreatening form in a few US news sources.

The *Washington Post* found an economics professor at the University of Wisconsin to provide reassurances that it was "not really a credible threat" that China would intervene in currency or bond markets in any way that could hurt the dollar's value or raise US interest rates, because China would hurt its own pocketbook by such actions.

US Treasury Secretary Henry Paulson, just back from Beijing, where he gave China orders to raise the value of the Chinese yuan [Chinese dollar] "without delay," dismissed the Chinese announcement as "frankly absurd."

Both the professor and the Treasury Secretary are greatly mistaken.

Statements by the Chinese

First, understand that the announcement was not made by a minister or vice minister of the government. The Chinese government is inclined to have important announcements come

Paul Craig Roberts, "One Big Reason Markets Are Plunging: China's Threat to the Dollar Is Real," *Counterpunch*, August 9, 2007. www.counterpunch.org/roberts08102007 .html. Reproduced by permission.

from research organizations that work closely with the government. This announcement came from two such organizations. A high official of the Development Research Center, an organization with cabinet rank, let it be known that US financial stability was too dependent on China's financing of US red ink for the US to be giving China orders. An official at the Chinese Academy of Social Sciences pointed out that the reserve currency status of the US dollar was dependent on China's good will as America's lender.

What the two officials said is completely true. It is something that some of us have known for a long time. What is different is that China publicly called attention to Washington's dependence on China's good will. By doing so, China signaled that it was not going to be bullied or pushed around.

The Chinese made no threats. To the contrary, one of the officials said, "China doesn't want any undesirable phenomenon in the global financial order." The Chinese message is different. The message is that Washington does not have hegemony over Chinese policy, and if matters go from push to shove, Washington can expect financial turmoil.

China Could Afford to Lose Its Dollar Holdings

Paulson can talk tough, but the Treasury has no foreign currencies with which to redeem its debt. The way the Treasury pays off the bonds that come due is by selling new bonds, a hard sell in a falling market deserted by the largest buyer.

American economists make a mistake in their reasoning when they assume that China needs large reserves of foreign exchange.

Paulson found solace in his observation that the large Chinese holdings of US Treasuries comprise only "one day's trading volume in Treasuries." This is a meaningless comparison.

If the supply suddenly doubled, does Paulson think the price of Treasuries would not fall and the interest rate not rise? If Paulson believes that US interest rates are independent of China's purchases and holdings of Treasuries, [President George W.] Bush had better quickly find himself a new Treasury Secretary.

Now let's examine the University of Wisconsin economist's opinion that China cannot exercise its power because it would result in losses on its dollar holdings. It is true that if China were to bring any significant percentage of its holdings to market, or even cease to purchase new Treasury issues, the prices of bonds would decline, and China's remaining holdings would be worth less. The question, however, is whether this is of any consequence to China, and, if it is, whether this cost is greater or lesser than avoiding the cost that Washington is seeking to impose on China.

The notion that China cannot exercise its power without losing its US markets is wrong. American consumers are as dependent on imports . . . from China as they are on imported oil.

American economists make a mistake in their reasoning when they assume that China needs large reserves of foreign exchange. China does not need foreign exchange reserves for the usual reasons of supporting its currency's value and paying its trade bills. China does not allow its currency to be traded in currency markets. Indeed, there are not enough yuan available to trade. Speculators, betting on the eventual rise of the yuan's value, are trying to capture future gains by trading "virtual yuan." The other reason is that China does not have foreign trade deficits, and does not need reserves in other currencies with which to pay its bills. Indeed, if China had creditors, the creditors would be pleased to be paid in yuan as the currency is thought to be undervalued.

Despite China's support of the Treasury bond market, China's large holdings of dollar-denominated financial instruments have been depreciating for some time as the dollar declines against other traded currencies, because people and central banks in other countries are either reducing their dollar holdings or ceasing to add to them. China's dollar holdings reflect the creditor status China acquired when US corporations offshored their production to China. Reportedly, 70 per cent of the goods on Wal-Mart's shelves are made in China. China has gained technology and business knowhow from the US firms that have moved their plants to China. China has large coastal cities, choked with economic activity and traffic, that make America's large cities look like country towns. China has raised about 300 million of its population into higher living standards, and is now focusing on developing a massive internal market some 4 to 5 times more populous than America's.

The notion that China cannot exercise its power without losing its US markets is wrong. American consumers are as dependent on imports of manufactured goods from China as they are on imported oil. In addition, the profits of US brand name companies are dependent on the sale to Americans of the products that they make in China. The US cannot, in retaliation, block the import of goods and services from China without delivering a knock-out punch to US companies and US consumers. China has many markets and can afford to lose the US market easier than the US can afford to lose the American brand names on Wal-Mart's shelves that are made in China. Indeed, the US is even dependent on China for advanced technology products. If truth be known, so much US production has been moved to China that many items on which consumers depend are no longer produced in America.

The Cost to China of Raising Its Currency Value

Now let's consider the cost to China of dumping dollars or Treasuries compared to the cost that the US is trying to impose on China. If the latter is higher than the former, it pays China to exercise the "nuclear option" and dump the dollar.

The US wants China to revalue the yuan, that is, to make the dollar value of the yuan higher. Instead of a dollar being worth 8 yuan, for example, Washington wants the dollar to be worth only 5.5 yuan. Washington thinks that this would cause US exports to China to increase, as they would be cheaper for the Chinese, and for Chinese exports to the US to decline, as they would be more expensive. This would end, Washington thinks, the large trade deficit that the US has with China.

This way of thinking dates from pre-offshoring days. In former times, domestic and foreign-owned companies would compete for one another's markets, and a country with a lower valued currency might gain an advantage.

Today, however, about half of the so-called US imports from China are the offshored production of US companies for their American markets. The US companies produce in China, not because of the exchange rate, but because labor, regulatory, and harassment costs are so much lower in China. Moreover, many US firms have simply moved to China, and the cost of abandoning their new Chinese facilities and moving production back to the US would be very high.

When all these costs are considered, it is unclear how much China would have to revalue its currency in order to cancel its cost advantages and cause US firms to move enough of their production back to America to close the trade gap.

The Results of Revaluation

To understand the shortcomings of the statements by the Wisconsin professor and Treasury Secretary Paulson, consider that if China were to increase the value of the yuan by 30 percent, the value of China's dollar holdings would decline by 30 percent. It would have the same effect on China's pocketbook as dumping dollars and Treasuries in the markets.

Consider also, that as revaluation causes the yuan to move up in relation to the dollar (the reserve currency), it also causes the yuan to move up against every other traded currency. Thus, the Chinese cannot revalue as Paulson has ordered without making Chinese goods more expensive not merely to Americans but everywhere.

Compare this result with China dumping dollars. With the yuan pegged to the dollar, China can dump dollars without altering the exchange rate between the yuan and the dollar. As the dollar falls, the yuan falls with it. Goods and services produced in China do not become more expensive to Americans, and they become cheaper elsewhere. By dumping dollars, China expands its entry into other markets and accumulates more foreign currencies from trade surpluses.

Now consider the non-financial costs to China's self-image and rising prestige of permitting the US government to set the value of its currency. America's problems are of its own making, not China's. A rising power such as China is likely to prove a reluctant scapegoat for America's decades of abuse of its reserve currency status.

Economists and government officials believe that a rise in consumer prices by 30 per cent is good if it results from yuan revaluation, but that it would be terrible, even beyond the pale, if the same 30 percent rise in consumer prices resulted from a tariff put on goods made in China. The hard pressed American consumer would be hit equally hard either way. It is paradoxical that Washington is putting pressure on China to raise US consumer prices, while blaming China for harming Americans. As is usually the case, the harm we suffer is inflicted by Washington.

Trade with China Has Helped the U.S. Economy

Geoffrey Garrett

Geoffrey Garrett is president of the Pacific Council on International Policy and professor of international relations, business administration, communication and law at the University of Southern California.

In the heat of the Democratic race for the presidential nomination [in 2008], Senator Hillary Rodham Clinton summarized well the prevailing US sentiment about China: "China's steel comes here and our jobs go there. We play by the rules and they manipulate their currency."

But in reality, China is actually doing what America has long demanded on trade and exchange rates. In addition to reducing barriers to imports and export subsidies, Beijing has allowed the yuan [Chinese dollar] to appreciate significantly against the dollar—by more than 14 per cent since the middle of 2005.

So why isn't the Bush administration silencing the Democrats' China bashing by trumpeting this apparent exchange rate victory? It's because the bilateral trade deficit with China, which a stronger yuan was supposed to reduce, continues to hit all-time highs—US$256 billion last year [2007], a 10 per cent increase over 2006.

But playing to American insecurities about China is not the way to stabilize what will be the US' most important bilateral relationship over the next several decades. What the US needs is a new vision for its relations with Belling, one based on further economic integration, not protectionism. This is the best way to sustain America's long 20th century economic boom well into this century.

Geoffrey Garrett, "China Trade a Boon to US," *South China Morning Post*, March 19, 2008. Reprinted at www.pacificcouncil.org/pdfs/GG_oped_SCMP.pdf. Reproduced by permission.

The Trade Deficit Is Here to Stay

Here are three trade secrets that should inform a "straight talk" revolution in Washington where China is concerned. First, the trade deficit with China will not go away soon. But this has more to do with macroeconomics than trade barriers in China.

Chinese domestic investment has boomed over the past decade, while the US economy has been driven by consumer spending. China has bought hundreds of billions of dollars to keep its currency down. But this has helped keep US interest rates low, allowing Americans to buy homes and to borrow against the real estate appreciation they expected.

The US has benefited from the vast quantities of dollars and Treasury bills . . . China has purchased in recent years to manage the dollar-yuan exchange rate.

All these trends have now been reversed. Beijing has allowed the yuan to appreciate against the dollar. It has also put the brakes on domestic investment for fear that its economy is overheating. In the US, the subprime melt down has brought the economy to a near standstill in growth terms. The combined result of these abrupt macroeconomic reversals is that US exports to China have grown twice as quickly as Chinese exports to the US in the past two years.

So why does the US-China trade deficit continue to climb? The US exports to China less than one-fifth as much as it imports from China. The much faster growth on the much smaller exports base is still overwhelmed by the slower growth in the much larger import volume. Even if US exports continue to grow twice as quickly as imports from China, the bilateral deficit will increase for years to come.

But the rapid growth in US exports to China should be cause for celebration in the US. And rising Chinese imports provide affordable goods to Americans. Focusing on the trade deficit conceals this fact.

Chinese Imports Are U.S. Products

A second secret is that the bulk of Chinese exports to the US are not really made "by China." They are not even really "made in China." The Chinese economy today is in large measure an assembly platform for foreign firms to turn components designed and made elsewhere into final products, and then to export them to the rest of the world. More than 60 per cent of Chinese exports are in fact the sales outside China of multinationals operating in China.

Consider the iconic Apple iPod. Every iPod shipped from China and sold in the US adds to the country's trade deficit with China. But what Apple says on the back of every iPod is true: "designed by Apple in California, assembled in China" from chips, hard drives and screens made in the US, Korea and Japan. Chinese assembly adds only a tiny amount to the value of each iPod.

US manufacturing jobs are no doubt lost as a result. But these are in assembly—the lowest tech part of the production process. Jobs are also created, and they are in the highest tech and most innovative parts of the American economy—design, marketing, finance and logistics. This is not only a positive trade-off for the US economy, it is also positive for the US labour force.

Chinese Investments and U.S. Interest Rates

A final secret is that the US has benefited from the vast quantities of dollars and Treasury bills (estimated at three-quarters of a trillion dollars) China has purchased in recent years to manage the dollar-yuan exchange rate. Ample China-funded credit kept US interest rates low after September 11 [2001] and the dot-com bust, fuelling both consumer spending and the run-up in housing prices.

It is time for US leaders actually to lead on China, rather than pander to understandable insecurities in middle America. Turning trade secrets into widely understood facts of life is a very good place to start.

The U.S.-China Trade Deficit Will Be Short-Lived

Li Jin and Shan Li

Li Jin is assistant professor of finance at the Harvard Business School. Shan Li is vice chairman of China Overseas-Educated Scholars Development Foundation and the former chief executive officer of Bank of China International.

Is there another international conflict on America's horizon? Tension is steadily mounting between the United States and China over trade issues. The U.S. trade deficit with China accounted for almost one-third the record $765 billion U.S. trade deficit in 2006. Both sides agree that this large imbalance is unsustainable, but negotiations to reduce it are making little progress—putting pressure on the negotiators in Washington at this week's [May 22, 2007] Strategic Economic Dialogue meetings. If not managed properly, the trade imbalance could escalate into a trade war.

A Short-Lived Problem

But is this conflict really necessary? The U.S. economy is healthy, close to full employment and flexible. Over time, the U.S. will likely "grow out of the problem" of trade deficits with China, as former Fed [U.S. Federal Reserve, the U.S. Central Bank System] Chairman Alan Greenspan put it. As China's industrialization matures, its citizens will grow richer and domestic consumption will rise, thus enabling the country to achieve better balanced growth.

Still, some in Washington complain that the trade deficit has led to an unsustainable scenario where U.S. net debt now totals 20% of total GDP [gross domestic product, a measure

Li Jin and Shan Li, "The U.S.-China Trade Deficit, Debunked," *Wall Street Journal*, May 22, 2007. Reprinted with permission of *The Wall Street Journal*, as conveyed through Copyright Clearance Center, Inc.

of a country's total economic output]—a heavy interest burden. Large U.S. national debts financed by foreign central banks also increase the vulnerability of U.S. financial markets, as the money could be pulled out of the U.S. market at any time. In addition, many politicians have called for protectionist measures in the wake of the loss of three million U.S. manufacturing jobs since, 2001.

China's policy makers have worries, too. The country's rapidly increasing foreign exchange reserves—a result of its sustained large trade surplus and its open-market interventions to stabilize its exchange rate—have drastically increased the domestic money supply, leading to inflationary pressure and asset-market bubbles. In addition, the fast accumulation of Chinese foreign-exchange reserves has fueled speculation that China might eventually give in to the pressure and allow for a faster appreciation of the renminbi [Chinese currency] against the U.S. dollar. The ensuing speculative investment increases the cost for open-market intervention by the Chinese central bank.

The good news, as Mr. Greenspan and U.S. Treasury Secretary Henry Paulson have pointed out, is that the current trade imbalance is likely short-lived for both countries. Therefore, the real policy challenge is to find the most efficient solution to the bilateral trade imbalance in the short term. The solution provided by U.S. policy makers is to focus on the U.S. dollar-renminbi exchange rate. The [George W.] Bush administration and Congress are pressing China to appreciate the renminbi rapidly relative to the U.S. dollar. We think this is at best a suboptimal solution, with three major flaws.

Problems with an Exchange Rate Solution

First, this solution is not mutually agreeable and therefore unenforceable. A sharp appreciation of the renminbi would endanger China's export-dependent economy. The mainland is undergoing rapid industrialization to absorb over 300 million rural laborers into the industrial sector. An interruption to that process could cause considerable social instability in China—something the leaders in Beijing want to avoid. If the U.S. pushes too hard, it could lead to a trade war.

The fundamental problem of the exchange-rate focused solution is that it addresses the terms of trade, rather than trade itself.

On the surface, a trade war would damage the U.S. less than China: In 2006, the U.S. imported $288 billion of goods from China and only exported $55 billion. However, the collateral damage of the trade war would include foreign direct investment (FDI). While Chinese FDI in the U.S. is quite small, U.S. FDI in China is substantial and constitutes an important channel for American firms selling in China. Equally serious, a trade war might severely disrupt the flow of Chinese trade-surplus funds into U.S. financial markets, particularly government bond markets. Such flow has in recent years been instrumental in propping up U.S. Treasury bond markets, especially as the low returns on U.S. government bonds make them less attractive to private sector investors.

Secondly, this solution fails to recognize the fact that the trade imbalance between the two countries is a multilateral, not a bilateral, issue. China serves as the final assembly point for a significant portion of the U.S.-bound exports of other Asian economies. In fact, China runs a substantial trade deficit with its Asian neighbors, suggesting that countries like Japan and Korea are using China to assemble goods, then export them to the U.S. China's trade surplus with the U.S. actually represents the trade surplus of the region—a fact that undermines renminbi appreciation alone as a remedy for the trade imbalance. A unilateral appreciation of the renminbi would likely shift Asian countries' assembly plants to other low-cost Asian countries, not back to America.

Last but not least, this solution may create huge risks for U.S. financial markets. It is widely believed that a unilateral appreciation of renminbi against the dollar would not correct the U.S. trade deficit, given that China's deficit accounted for $233 billion as of the end of last year [2006]. For the exchange-rate adjustment to be effective in resolving the U.S. trade deficit, a substantial dollar depreciation would be necessary. Such a move might trigger a massive exodus of foreign central bank reserve assets from the U.S. treasury market, sharply reducing the demand for U.S. treasury securities and increasing U.S. interest rates—at a huge cost to the U.S. economy and crucial elements in it, such as the housing market.

Alternative Solutions

We think the fundamental problem of the exchange-rate focused solution is that it addresses the terms of trade, rather than trade itself. If both the U.S. and China move one step back and focus their negotiation on trade rather than exchange rates, they may find ample room to restore the trade balance amicably.

The two economies are complementary rather than competitive, at least in the foreseeable future.

Specifically, the U.S. may consider loosening restrictions on technology exports to China, where U.S. companies are losing out to their Japanese and European competitors. The U.S. harbors reasonable concerns about limiting military-use technology exports to China, but there are vast areas of non-military use technology exports—particularly environmental protection and energy-efficiency technologies—that China desperately needs.

For its part, China might consider levying environmental and energy taxation on its exports, to properly account for the burden of the export sector to the environment and energy consumption. This is in fact consistent with China's domestic policy to maintain sustainable economic growth.

China could also actively invest its newly generated trade surplus directly in the U.S. in the form of FDI, since this prevents the trade surplus from entering China's financial markets and fueling the oversupply of domestic liquidity. It also helps create jobs in the U.S., and yields a potentially higher return than an investment in U.S. Treasury securities. Such direct investment would be welcomed by the U.S. In 2005, FDI in the U.S. created jobs for over five million American workers and provided 4.5% of all private-sector jobs.

Of course, China should still take more action on its exchange rate even though it is not at the core of our proposed solution for the trade imbalance. China should allow for reasonably faster appreciation of its currency to the extent that the Chinese economy can tolerate it. This could not only help further reduce the bilateral trade deficit, but also help decouple the renminbi from the U.S. dollar's exchange rate—giving China more independence in managing its domestic monetary policy, while giving the U.S. flexibility, too.

China aspires to be the world's leading manufacturing center, while the U.S. wants to maintain its leadership position in R&D [research and development] and financial markets. As such, the two economies are complementary rather than competitive, at least in the foreseeable future. Instead of short-sighted posturing, cautious policies on both sides should be able to sustain growth and enhance cooperation. Confrontation is in no one's interest.

The United States Should Appreciate the Cheap Goods from China

Michelle Bussenius

Michelle Bussenius is the editor of Focus on Issues, *a publication of the Hoover Institution, a public policy research center at Stanford University devoted to the study of politics, economics, and international affairs.*

Despite consumer concerns about "tainted" products from China, calls from media pundits to put tighter controls on Chinese imports, and presidential candidates from both parties stumping on related issues, Americans continue buying imports from China at record rates. Retail outlets continue to provide vast quantities of Chinese-manufactured goods; buyers spent more than $266 billion on those goods between January and October 2007. The point of contention, however, is that, during the same period in 2007, the United States exported $52 billion worth of goods to China—which continues to draw the attention and ire of politicians and pundits.

Running a trade deficit with China is nothing new—U.S. imports from that country have outweighed its exports since 1975. The deficit, only $6 million in 1985, has grown significantly during the [past] few decades. In the United States, those critical of the current U.S.-China trade relationship claim the growing deficit is due, in large part, to what they view as China's unfair trade practices and an intentionally undervalued renminbi ("people's currency"; the official currency of the People's Republic of China, the renminbi is also known as the yuan). According to critics, an undervalued renminbi results in Chinese exports being artificially cheap, thus raising China's trade surplus and reducing competition from other countries. In turn, some Chinese officials assert that the combination of a weakening dollar and tight U.S. control on the export of high-tech goods is partly responsible for the increasing deficit.

Tough Talk on Trade

In September 2006, U.S. president George W. Bush and Chinese president Hu Jintao created the Strategic Economic Dialogue. These twice-yearly meetings allow high-level leaders from both countries to discuss ways to jointly overcome economic challenges and ensure both equally benefit from the growing economic partnership. On December 11, 2007, the two-day talks reconvened outside Beijing, where U.S. treasury secretary Henry Paulson and his delegation met with their counterparts, led by Chinese vice premier Wu Yi.

During the meeting, the Chinese warned that U.S. protectionist measures, including a spate of congressional bills pressuring China to reform its currency and actively addressing the trade surplus, would exacerbate existing trade problems between the two countries. [U.S.] Commerce secretary Carlos Gutierrez contended the United States needs greater market access in China to counteract the trade imbalance; Paulson reiterated that China needs to step up efforts to appreciate its currency, saying that a fairly valued renminbi would help China offset its rising inflation and cool its overheated economy.

Some economists claim that the deficit with China costs American jobs. The Economic Policy Institute, a Washington-based think tank, claims that 1.8 million manufacturing jobs have been lost since China entered the World Trade Organization (WTO) [an international organization that regulates global trade] in 2001. Such statements fuel U.S. accusations that China is failing to live up to its WTO membership commitments.

U.S. presidential candidates are routinely grilled on their position on the deficit and on their ideas for "solving the trade deficit problem." But does the trade deficit truly spell potential doom for the U.S. economy? Although some economists raise concerns about China, others are less worried. Hoover research fellow Russell Roberts says that imports do not cost U.S. jobs "but rather that imports have the ability to destroy jobs in certain industries. But because trade allows us to buy goods more cheaply than we otherwise could, resources are freed up to expand existing opportunities and to create new ones." He contends that even though the United States has imported $6 trillion more in goods than it has exported since 1976, employment has increased by more than 40 million jobs during that same period.

"We should enjoy the flow of low-priced Chinese imports—this great deal won't last forever."

Few can argue the success of China's economic reform in 1978, which liberalized government controls over foreign trade and investment and encouraged the formation of private enterprise. China is now the world's fourth-largest economy, following, in order, the United States, Japan, and Germany. This year, China's economy grew by 11.4 percent over [2007], outperforming the United States, whose annual economic growth, according to a White House fact sheet issued in November 2007, has averaged 2.8 percent since 2001.

Growing Pains

A relatively new player in the free market economy, China's explosive growth is not entirely devoid of growing pains. China's reliance on loans from state banks to finance its frenetic spending on new factories and technologies may implode if industries such as auto manufacturing and steel production are unable to make a profit as a result of overcapacity. Likewise, there is growing international pressure for China to appreciate its currency (1 U.S. dollar is currently equal to 7.38 renminbi) to its real value. Skeptics point out that there is no "real value" to the currency and that those demands are simply a way of protecting U.S. industries from foreign competition at the expense of U.S. consumers. Chinese officials, including Vice Commerce Minister Chen Deming, oppose rapidly appreciating the renminbi, saying that appreciation of the Chinese currency would not help ease the trade imbalance between China and the United States.

Despite momentary disagreements and terse words over exports and the renminbi, many economists believe that China is well on its way to becoming an economic powerhouse on par with the G-7 nations [France, Germany, Italy, Japan, Canada, United Kingdom, and United States]. Although the future tenor of U.S.-China trade relations is likely to include more than a few challenges, Robert J. Barro, senior fellow at the Hoover Institution, takes an optimistic approach: "We should avoid the protectionist policies that now seem so threatening. And we should enjoy the flow of low-priced Chinese imports—this great deal won't last forever."

CHAPTER 4

Should the United States Toughen Its Trade Policy Toward China?

Chapter Overview

Mark Trumbull

Mark Trumbull is a staff writer for the Christian Science Monitor.

The [George W.] Bush administration faces congressional pressure to act—not just talk—to address a widening trade imbalance between the two nations [the United States and China].

For just the first three months of the year [2007], Chinese exports to the United States exceeded imports by $57 billion. That's nearly one-third of America's overall trade deficit with the world. It's up sharply from five years ago, when the first-quarter trade gap with China was $19 billion, or about one-fifth of the trade imbalance.

Differing Opinions on Remedies

Many economists agree that the US trade deficit is reaching levels that can't, and won't, be sustainable for the long term. But a key question, embodied in the current differences between a restive Congress and the Bush administration, is what to do about it.

Some say that the proposed fixes could be worse than the problem. One bill recently introduced in Congress would slap new import tariffs on Chinese goods, a penalty for alleged currency manipulation that favors Chinese exports to America.

"The imposition of a tax [such as a tariff] is a poor way to go about trying to resolve" differences with China, says Michael Cosgrove, an economist at the University of Dallas. "We end up hurting somebody else here at home."

For one thing, a law that penalizes Chinese imports could make consumer goods more expensive in the US. Many busi-

Mark Trumbull, "How to Tackle Trade Deficit with China," *Christian Science Monitor*, May 22, 2007. www.csmonitor.com/2007/0522/p03s03-usec.html. Reproduced by permission from Christian Science Monitor (www.csmonitor.com).

nesses, too, would face higher prices for products made partly in China. Other nations, moreover, might follow America's lead, making the world less open to the commerce that has helped fuel several years of strong global growth.

That's one reason [U.S.] Treasury Secretary Henry Paulson and his Chinese counterpart, Wu Yi, are stressing patience and diplomacy. . . . "The win-win nature of this [trade] relationship is amply demonstrated by the rapid growth of bilateral trade," Vice Premier Wu wrote [in 2007] in *The Wall Street Journal.*

Issues of Concern

But while [U.S.-China] talks represent the goal of long-term engagement, short-term tensions are bound to be a focus as well.

Speaking to students at the Harvard Business School in Boston earlier this month [May 2007], Secretary Paulson acknowledged that the "strategic economic dialogue," launched by both nations [in 2006], faces pressure. "If you don't get some short-term results, you'll never get to the long term," he said.

Supporters of a stronger yuan . . . say it would . . . make US exports more competitively priced in Asian markets [and curb] American demand for Asian imports.

Several issues are of central concern. One is the protection of intellectual property, everything from patents to copyrights on music and movies. Another is alleged subsidies in violation of US trade statutes. The value of the yuan [Chinese dollar] looms the largest for many China critics, because it affects the terms of trade across all categories of goods. [In May 2007], China agreed to allow its currency to fluctuate within a wider band of values, but said this did not necessarily mean the currency would be allowed to rise significantly.

Sen. Charles Schumer [Democrat] of New York was quick to voice skepticism about the move. "This is a nice gesture, but in the past, most of their gestures have not produced any concrete change," he said in a statement. "The Chinese should recognize that they face the prospect of strong WTO [World Trade Organization, an international organization that regulates global trade]-compliant legislation if there isn't significant progress."

Any countervailing measures against China, designed to punish and deter unfair trade practices, must be able to pass muster with the World Trade Organization, the ultimate arbiter for its 150 member nations.

A higher yuan, over time, could be difficult for the US economy. Chinese imports would cost more for US consumers. Economists say that other Asian nations would probably allow their currencies to float higher as well. That could push up inflation.

But supporters of a stronger yuan, including labor unions and many small manufacturers, say it would also make US exports more competitively priced in Asian markets. And if it curbs American demand for Asian imports, that could help the US economy shift to a more sustainable path. They say America now imports too much and saves too little money.

"We need to proceed on several fronts," says Robert Scott, a trade expert at the Economic Policy Institute, a labor-allied research group in Washington. The White House has "been almost completely silent on this issue until just this year [2007] when the Democrats took control of Congress." He urges stronger action by the administration to penalize China for illegal subsidies and more pressure to remove Chinese barriers to US exports, as well as addressing currency manipulation.

It's not clear whether legislation will pass in the current Congress, but analysts say the prospects have improved with the Democratic victories in last fall's [2006] elections.

The Fair Currency Act of 2007, the proposed measure to penalize "exchange-rate misalignment," has 100 bipartisan co-sponsors led by Reps. Tim Ryan (D) of Ohio and Duncan Hunter (R) of California.

The tussling is not just between Congress and President Bush, but between global corporations and domestic interests.

China's export growth has been propelled by multinational corporations. Exports of foreign affiliates operating in China—mainly US and European companies—accounted for 58 percent of Chinese exports in 2006, up from 40 percent in 1996, according to research by Bank of America in New York.

These companies are generally reaping big profits in China and see much to gain by growing international trade. Hotly debated, however, is whether such trade has done much for US workers. "Corporate interest has diverged from the national interest," says Mr. Scott.

It Is Time to Reduce the Trade Deficit with China

Peter Morici

Peter Morici is a professor at the University of Maryland School of Business and former chief economist at the U.S. International Trade Commission during the Bill Clinton Administration.

Americans need to knock down some false gods. Globalization is not an unalloyed good. We don't need 300-horsepower cars. And Wall Street is not a citadel of integrity.

The 1990s were the golden age of free trade. The U.S. sealed the North American Free Trade Agreement, launched the World Trade Organization and escorted China into that temple of global commerce.

The idea was simple: Americans would import more T-shirts and furniture and sell more industrial machinery and software to a world hungry for technology. Americans would move into higher-productivity export industries and earn higher incomes in the trade-off.

The Effects of Free Trade

In the 2000s, America's CEOs, bankers and management consultants learned how to outsource just about everyone's job but their own. Radiologists who read MRIs, journalists who wrote copy for local papers and computer engineers joined the ranks of workers displaced by imports.

The average American worker's income stagnated, and, for many, inflation-adjusted wages fell. U.S. productivity gains were hogged by executives at Wall Street banks, technology companies and multinationals through big bonuses and peculiar, can't-lose stock options.

Peter Morici, "It's Time to Cut the Trade Deficit," *Forbes.com*, March 26, 2008. www.forbes.com/opinions/2008/03/25/globalization-recession-bernanke-banks-oped-cx_pm_0326morici.html. © 2008 Forbes.com LLC. Reprinted by permission of FORBES.com.

The rest of us sunk into debt to fill our gas tanks, feed our children and, admittedly, buy too many cheap imports at Wal-Mart.

Imports soared much more rapidly than exports, the annual trade deficit jumped to more than $700 billion and Americans borrowed more than $6 trillion from foreigners to pay for two decades of trade deficits. This math permitted Americans to consume much more than we produced and spend more than we earned.

China is perhaps the biggest renegade in the mugging of the American middle class. The U.S. has slashed tariffs on Chinese products from auto parts to TVs, while China maintains much higher tariffs and notorious regulatory restrictions for U.S. exports in its market.

Topping it all, China subsidizes foreign purchases of its currency, the yuan, to the tune of $460 billion a year, making its products cheap on U.S. store shelves. The U.S. annual trade deficit with China is about $250 billion.

Chinese growth has pushed up global petroleum prices nearly five fold in six years [since 2002], and the U.S. oil deficit is now $350 billion and rising.

The U.S. Economy Falters

The banks came up with more creative and risky mortgage products that permitted Americans to live beyond their means. We went from 10% down to 5% down to nothing down, with banks lending home buyers closing costs through second trusts.

Getting out of this mess is going to require Americans to live within their means—a.k.a. cut the trade deficit.

Some loans that required no payback for five years even let folks dig deeper in their pockets on the premise that home prices would always go up. The banks sold these risky loans, bundled as bonds, to foreign investors like the Chinese government and foreign pension funds, as well as to U.S. insurance companies and corporations with cash to park. The bank executives paid themselves like royalty for the privilege of bilking trusting clients. When the worst of the bonds—those backed by [risky] adjustable rate mortgages—collapsed, the banks got stuck with billions of unsold bonds.

Most recently, Bear Stearns [large global investment bank] collapsed, and the U.S. Federal Reserve [the Fed, the U.S. central banking system] is lending the banks $600 billion against shaky bonds on a 90-day revolving basis. That essentially socializes the banks' losses on bad bonds.

You have to love Ben Bernanke's [head of the Federal Reserve] free trade capitalism. If you are an autoworker put out of work by Korean imports, he, as a good economist, tells you to go to school and find other work. If you are a New York banker caught paying yourself too much and run short of foreign investors to fleece, Ben will make you a loan and keep rolling until the bank finds a new game.

Now foreign investors are getting nervous about all the money they have loaned Americans and the integrity of U.S. banks. They are fleeing dollar investments for euro-denominated securities, gold, oil and just about anything more tangible than the shaky greenback.

Americans are forced to cut back, not just on purchases of cheap Chinese coffee makers, but also on automobiles and other products made in the U.S. Falling demand is casting the U.S. economy into recession, and we won't be able to borrow enough to pull ourselves out.

Fixing the Mess

Getting out of this mess is going to require Americans to live within their means—a.k.a. cut the trade deficit—and throw out the rascals on Wall Street. Cutting the trade deficit requires burning less gasoline and balancing commerce with China.

Americans must either let the price of gas double to force conservation or accept cars with tougher mileage standards. Fifty miles per gallon by 2020, instead of the 35 required by current law, is achievable, but that means more hybrids and lighter vehicles.

The U.S. government should tax dollar-yuan conversions at a rate equal to China's subsidies on yuan purchases until China stops manipulating currency markets. That would reduce imports from China, move a lot of production back home, raise U.S. productivity and workers incomes, and reduce the federal budget deficit.

Ben Bernanke has given the banks a lot and received little in return—except a lot of bad loans on the Fed's books. It is high time he condition the Fed's largesse on reforms at the big banks, even if that means lower salaries for the Brahmins on Wall Street.

After all, what makes them so special?

The United States Should Take Action Against China's Mercantilist Practices

Howard Richman, Raymond Richman, and Jesse Richman

Howard Richman, Raymond Richman, and Jesse Richman are instructors of Internet economics, public and international affairs, and political science, respectively. They are the authors of Trading Away Our Future: How to Fix Our Government-Driven Trade Deficits and Faulty Tax System Before It's Too Late.

At a press conference on April 29 [2008], President [George W.] Bush issued a gloomy assessment of the U.S. economy, saying the nation is in for "very difficult times, very difficult." The next day, the Commerce Department released preliminary statistics for the first quarter of 2008. Real GDP [gross domestic product, a measure of a country's economic output] was up at a paltry annual rate of just 0.6 percent for the second quarter in a row, investment in the American economy was down for the eighth quarter in a row, and the trade deficit was worse for the second quarter in a row.

China's Mercantilist Policies

The worsening trade deficit was especially disheartening since most economists had expected that the plunging dollar on world currency markets would improve the U.S. trade deficit by making American goods less expensive abroad and foreign goods more expensive here. Indeed, the trade deficit probably would be in decline if more of America's trading partners played fair. Unfortunately, they don't.

To understand the dilemma, consider the situation faced by Tim Sullivan, CEO of Bucyrus International [a U.S. Company]. The Chinese government just slapped a 40 percent tariff on the heavy mining equipment Bucyrus makes in Wisconsin and exports to China. That tariff is only a small part of the strategy used by China to keep expanding their trade deficit with the United States. Coupled with systematic protectionism, the Chinese government has used its yuan [Chinese dollar] to buy more than a trillion dollars in order to "sterilize" them so they wouldn't be used by Chinese citizens to buy American products. In this way, they bid down the yuan and bid up the dollar to keep Chinese wages low compared to American wages. More and more countries are joining China in this mercantilist strategy of selling to the United States without buying, originally invented by Japan shortly after World War II. The technical name for this strategy is mercantilism, a practice denounced by economists beginning with Adam Smith in 1776.

The Bush administration has abysmally mismanaged U.S. trade policy.

If it weren't for these mercantilist policies, American manufacturing companies like Bucyrus International would be opening new ultra-modern factories in the United States in order to sell to the rapidly growing Chinese economy and other rapidly expanding world markets. Instead, American manufacturing companies are laying off employees. The latest *Employment Situation Summary* from the Bureau of Labor Statistics reports that 46,000 jobs were lost in the U.S. manufacturing sector in April [2008] alone. Of these lost jobs, 17,000 were in our motor vehicles and parts sector, partly as a result of China's 30 percent tariffs on foreign-made vehicles and auto parts. Many of these laid-off manufacturing workers will take more poorly paying jobs in the service sector, causing real U.S. median income to fall further, just as it has been doing since President Bush first took office in 2000.

U.S. Trade Policy

The Bush administration has abysmally mismanaged U.S. trade policy. We hope that the next administration learns from its mistakes. President Bush's solution to the worsening U.S. trade deficit with China was talk. That's right. His strategy was talk, talk, talk; journalists call it "jawboning." In December 2006, President Bush sent our government's top five financial leaders to China to convince the Chinese to mend their ways and allow the yuan to appreciate against the dollar. But, in 2007 our trade deficit with China worsened yet again to $252 billion from $229 billion the previous year. Talking loudly while carrying no stick doesn't work.

Unfortunately, the current presidential candidates are not proposing anything better:

- Sen. McCain takes a perverse pride in losing elections, such as the Michigan primary, by telling manufacturing workers that their "jobs aren't coming back." If he continues to advocate Bush's failed trade policies, he will lose Ohio, a "must-win" Republican state in November [2008].

- Sen. Obama's principal solution (Bush redux): jawboning by our diplomats. He says, "As president, I'll use all the diplomatic avenues open to me to insist that China stop manipulating its currency."

- Sen. Clinton's husband did nothing about the worsening trade deficits during his presidency. Although she correctly identifies many of the problems in our trade with China, she does not yet have substantive proposals that would actually improve the trade deficits.

Sens. Obama and Clinton both point to their having added their names as cosponsors to the bipartisan Currency Rate

Oversight Reform Act as evidence that they would get tough with China. Although a step in the right direction, this bill does not go far enough. According to the China Currency Coalition, "The processes set forth in the bill are too lengthy and uncertain to meet the urgent need to address the China currency problem in the short term."

Solutions

The American people are still waiting for a presidential candidate to propose something that would work. In our book, *Trading Away Our Future*, we suggest that the president announce to all the mercantilist countries that effective immediately their deficit on goods and services will have to be reduced by 20 percent per year. They may respond to this challenge by planning to increase their imports from us, reduce their exports to us, or some combination of both.

Failure to meet this annual goal would result in our imposition of a requirement that all imports from the offending country would require an Import Certificate purchased from the U.S. Treasury Department. Over a period of five years, the Treasury Department would steadily reduce the amount of available Import Certificates so that the targeted country's exports to the United States would be no higher than 5 percent above their imports from the United States.

These Import Certificates would be in full compliance with international rules. Article IV of the International Monetary Fund agreement specifically outlaws currency manipulations. Article 12 of the Uruguay Round General Agreement on Tariffs and Trade (GATT) [the predecessor to the current World Trade Organization trade system] specifically lets countries running a threatening overall trade deficit restrict imports from any country with whom they are running a trade deficit.

This plan would result in an immediate surge of investment in American manufacturing production. Both U.S. and foreign companies would start building new highly-efficient factories in the United States for export to China and other growing world markets. American wages would again head up, as would American median incomes.

The United States Should Crack Down on China's Unfair Trade Practices

Hillary for President

Hillary for President is the campaign Web site for Senator Hillary Clinton, a Democratic candidate for president in 2008 who was defeated in the Democratic presidential primary by Senator Barack Obama.

Hillary Clinton . . . unveiled a new set of proposals to strengthen trade enforcement and crack down on China's unfair trade policies. . . . "We need solutions to fix our trade laws, build a strong manufacturing base, and stand up to China and say that unsafe toys and unfair currency practices are unacceptable," said Clinton. "I know what manufacturing means for this country. It means good jobs, thriving communities and the products that keep this country going and growing every single day. Our manufacturers and manufacturing workers have shaped our past—and you will drive our future. And if you give me the chance, I will stand strong for you every single day as President."

Clinton's Proposal

As President, Hillary announced that she would provide relief for U.S. industries that have been hurt by excessive Chinese imports; aggressively use the World Trade Organization (WTO) [an international organization that regulates trade] to challenge other countries for violating trade rules; create a new Intellectual Property Enforcement Network to crack down on piracy issues; accept and review petitions when outside groups petition the government to enforce trade laws; and en-

Hillary for President, "Press Release: Hillary Clinton Calls for Stepped Up Enforcement of Trade Laws," hillaryclinton.com, April 14, 2008. www.hillaryclinton.com/news/release/view/?id=7089. Reproduced by permission.

sure that we can take retaliatory action against China and other non-market economies when they subsidize their domestic industries.

For too long, American workers have had a President who does not believe in enforcing our trade laws.

President [George W.] Bush has failed to effectively enforce our trade laws. For seven years [since 2001], the Bush Administration has ignored or under-utilized legitimate trade enforcement tools as countries like China have violated trade rules and hurt U.S. manufacturers. The Bush Administration has brought less than half as many cases to the WTO as our trading partners have brought against the US. It has also dragged its feet in addressing China's currency manipulation and actively worked against efforts to provide legitimate relief to threatened U.S. industries. During this period, the trade deficit has nearly doubled to $708 billion and China's holdings of U.S. public debt has risen to almost $500 billion—over 10 percent of total public holdings. President Bush has allowed China to become America's banker, making it harder to promote our interests and push back against their unfair trade practices.

Senator Clinton understands that lax enforcement has contributed to a trade policy that is not working for American workers or the American economy. She has already outlined an ambitious trade agenda, including a trade time-out to review existing trade agreements and to formulate a new pro-worker trade policy; a detailed four-part plan to fix NAFTA [North American Free Trade Agreement]; and appointing a new Trade Prosecutor and doubling the trade enforcement budget at USTR [United States Trade Representative, the agency that advises on trade policy]. The plan she outlined . . . will ensure that, as we modernize and improve trade agreements and trade laws, those laws are effectively and aggressively enforced, and ensure that America's trading partners play by the rules. . . .

Enforcing Trade Laws

For too long, American workers have had a President who does not believe in enforcing our trade laws. Hillary will reverse that trend by actively using our trade enforcement tools to promote U.S. interests and by strengthening those tools to ensure that our trading partners play by the rules.

1. *Aggressively challenge illegal trading practices through the World Trade Organization (WTO) Dispute Settlement Mechanism.* The Bush Administration has filed less than 3 cases a year at the WTO to challenge our trading partners for breaking WTO rules. That compares to an average of 11 cases filed per year during the [Bill] Clinton Administration. President Bush waited almost seven years before challenging some of China's most obvious trade violations, including on illegal subsidies and intellectual property rights. Meanwhile, our trading partners have been actively pursuing claims against the U.S. at the WTO, filing an average of seven cases per year since 2001. This puts the U.S. on its heels, and puts U.S. workers and businesses at a competitive disadvantage.

As President, Senator Clinton will fully utilize the WTO Dispute Settlement Mechanism to challenge practices that violate WTO commitments. For example, according to the National Trade Estimate, China continues to employ discriminatory regulations, subsidies, and import and export restrictions that may violate WTO rules, but which the U.S. is not adequately pursuing at the WTO. In addition, Hillary will work toward establishing WTO rules and policies that respect and strengthen workers' human rights and protect the environment. And she will work to speed up the decision making process at the WTO. Right now, the lengthy deliberation process means our industries continue to incur major losses during the time it takes to resolve a complaint.

2. Ensure that "Section 301" Petitions Alleging Unfair Trading Practices Receive a Fair, Nonpartisan Review. Another important tool in our trade enforcement toolkit is the provision that allows non-governmental actors to petition the government about unfair trading practices by our trading partners. The Bush Administration has failed to utilize this tool. Since President Bush took office, the United States Trade Representative has not only refused to take action based on the five Section 301 petitions that have been filed—it has refused to even open an investigation to find out if our industries are being treated unfairly. The Administration rejected without adequate explanation a petition filed by the AFL-CIO [American Federation of Labor and Congress of Industrial Organizations] detailing worker rights abuses in China, including the prohibition of independent union organizing, failure to enforce minimum wage and maximum hour regulations, and the use of child and forced labor. And the Administration dismissed a petition from 20 industrial, labor, agricultural, and service organizations on China's currency manipulation only a few hours after it was submitted.

With our trade deficit with China now at a record $256 billion, Hillary believes it is time for aggressive action to crack down on China's unfair trade practices.

As President, Senator Clinton will direct her USTR to investigate and publicly report on all Section 301 petitions that are filed, rather than dismissing them out of hand. She believes that Section 301 petitions deserve a fair, nonpartisan review, and should be followed up with appropriate action through our trade laws or at the WTO based on the outcome of the inquiry. She will ensure that this trade enforcement tool is used to help American workers and industries, not left by the wayside.

3. *Create an Intellectual Property Enforcement Network to stop IPR [Intellectual Property Rights] violations.* Studies have found that counterfeiting is an enormous business in China, costing the global intellectual property industry over $450 billion. In the US, over 81 percent of border seizures of products that violate IPR laws come from China. The US auto industry alone loses over $12 billion a year—at a cost equivalent to hiring 250,000 additional American workers—from counterfeits, 75 percent for which China is responsible. Senator Clinton understands that this is not a problem that can be fixed overnight. But she recognizes the importance of having a President that is willing to deploy diplomatic, legal and enforcement efforts to help reduce incidences of China's intellectual property rights abuses.

As President, Senator Clinton will create a new Intellectual Property Enforcement Network to develop and implement a comprehensive national effort to strengthen IPR protections. The IPEN [Intellectual Property Rights Enforcement Act], an idea championed by [Indiana] Senator [Evan] Bayh, would improve inter-agency coordination and create a new international task force to work with foreign governments on IPR enforcement. In addition, Hillary will increase the ITC's [International Trade Commission, a U.S. agency that provides trade advice] capacity to manage technologically complex IPR cases, including by allowing IPR experts to decide cases.

As a condition for China's entry into the WTO, the U.S. adopted special safeguard provisions that offer relief to industries hurt by excessive surges of Chinese imports.

Addressing China's Unfair Trade Practices

With our trade deficit with China now at a record $256 billion, Hillary believes it is time for aggressive action to crack down on China's unfair trade practices. Hillary Clinton will not take a passive line on unfair trade practices and will work to level the playing field for American workers, reducing our trade deficit and keeping more jobs here at home.

1. *Take a Tough Line on Currency Manipulation.* Foreign countries manipulate their currencies to make American goods expensive in their markets and to make their own goods artificially inexpensive. This practice hurts American workers and domestic producers, and it must end. Hillary is a co-sponsor of legislation that will require the administration to take definitive steps to stop China and other countries from harming American interests by undervaluing their currencies.

As President, she will move aggressively to address currency manipulation in China and other countries. Hillary has supported legislation to take one or more of the following actions to pressure China to revalue its currency, and will consider all of these actions as President: 1) adjusting export prices to account for the price distortion caused by currency misalignment; 2) disallowing the federal government to purchase products or services from China; 3) directing U.S. banks to pause in issuing loans to China; 4) pressuring the IMF [International Monetary Fund, an international financial organization] to consult with China; and/or 5) imposing a 27.5 percent tariff on all Chinese goods.

2. *Enforce "Section 421" Relief for U.S. Industries Hurt by Surges of Chinese Imports.* As a condition for China's entry into the WTO, the U.S. adopted special safeguard provisions that offer relief to industries hurt by excessive surges of Chinese imports. Yet since 2001, President Bush has completely abandoned a commitment to enforce this provision, known as "Section 421." In every instance that the International Trade Commission (ITC) has found a violation of Section 421 and recommended relief for U.S. manufacturers, the Bush Administration has blocked relief. These denials have not only handicapped deserving manufacturers—including in the steel industry—they have undermined trust and confidence in our trade laws and our capacity to stand up to China.

As President, Senator Clinton will restore the spirit and the letter of our China safeguard trade law by providing relief when the ITC makes a legitimate finding that a surge of Chinese imports is harming U.S. industries. She will require that hers and subsequent Administrations accept ITC findings, or present a public report on the reasons for denying such relief. In instances where relief is denied, Congress should have the authority to review and override such decisions by joint congressional resolution.

3. *Apply Countervailing Duties to Non-Market Economies Like China.* Under established policy, the U.S does not apply countervailing duties to non-market economies like China. This means that even when countries like China systematically subsidize their domestic export industries, the U.S. is lacking an important set of tools to apply leverage and help our domestic manufacturers compete. In March 2007—after 3.16 million manufacturing workers had already lost their jobs under President Bush's watch—the Commerce Department finally decided they would be willing to apply U.S. anti-subsidy law to imports from China. Yet this preliminary decision could be revoked at any point, which undermines the effectiveness of this trade enforcement tool in ensuring that China play by the rules.

Senator Clinton believes we should change the law once and for all so that countervailing duties can be applied to non-market economies. This change will help U.S. trade negotiators enforce our trade laws and help lessen unfair export subsidization so that our industries can compete on a level playing field.

The United States Must Level the Playing Field with China

Peter Navarro

Peter Navarro is a business professor at the University of California, Irvine and author of The Coming China Wars.

Why is China's economy booming even as the United States' economy slips deeper into recession? The presidential candidate that answers this question will not only cure America's economic woes but also capture the White House.

Policies That Do Not Work

Monetary policy differences clearly don't explain the growing divergence between a fast-growing China and a slow-growing United States. In fact, the central banks of both countries have failed miserably. China's central bank has repeatedly raised interest rates to slow down its economy and contain inflationary pressures—but its boom continues. In sharp contrast, the U.S. Federal Reserve has slashed interest rates, but the result has not been faster growth but merely an incredibly shrinking dollar.

Because U.S. monetary policy has failed miserably, a growing chorus is calling for fiscal stimulus. The front-running Democratic [presidential candidates for 2008] all urge increased government spending. Bowing to relentless Democratic pressure, President [George W.] Bush now wants a tax cut.

The Democratic proposals are populism run amok. Increased government spending will exacerbate the budget deficit. Because spending hikes move slowly through Congress, their effects typically show up too late—after the recession is over—and often spark inflation.

Peter Navarro, "It's the Economy, Comrade," *SFGate.com*, January 20, 2008. Reproduced by permission of the author.

The proposed new Bush tax cut is equally irresponsible. It, too, would exacerbate the budget deficit—which is largely the result of previous Bush tax cuts! A tax cut probably wouldn't provide adequate stimulus either. Consumers fearful of a prolonged recession are more likely to save their tax-cut money rather than spend it.

Reviving U.S. Industry

These observations bring us back to the question: Why is China booming as the U.S. stagnates? The answer is painfully obvious: America has lost millions of high-paying manufacturing jobs to China. This has vastly improved the fortunes of workers from Beijing and Shanghai to Guangzhou and Chongqing. However, the middle class of American heavy-industry cities such as Akron, Ohio, Detroit and Gary, Ind., have been hollowed out and are on life support. It's not just the "rust belt" suffering. From Silicon Valley's high-tech manufacturing and the South's textile mills and furniture factories to the Northeast's electronics industries, the China effect is taking its heavy recessionary toll. . . .

If we truly want to restore the health of the American economy, we must resuscitate our once dominant manufacturing sector and reclaim those jobs lost to China.

For those who scoff at such an idea, consider the U.S. steel industry. Through a remarkable technological makeover, this industry has increased its productivity by more than 50 percent in the course of the last decade while adding $350 billion to the economy and more than a million jobs.

Any U.S. manufacturing renaissance must also include leveling the playing field with China.

Other key manufacturing sectors—from aerospace, automotive and chemicals to cookware, plastics mold-building and semiconductors—are equally capable of such a transformation. Indeed, manufacturing has been the heart of American innovation, and no other country combines as many of the core requirements for a strong manufacturing base as ours—from economic and political freedom, the rule of law and property rights, and highly advanced capital markets to superior infrastructure and the world's most productive workforce.

To restore America's manufacturing might, we need well-funded education reforms to produce the skilled workers needed for American industry. We need precision-targeted tax policies to boost productivity; cost-cutting reforms that dramatically bring down health care, legal and regulatory costs; and a long overdue national energy policy that ensures plentiful and inexpensive energy.

Finally, we need a comprehensive technology policy to help U.S. manufacturers evolve to the next level of production and energy efficiencies. Here, we lag badly behind both Europe and Asia. Increased government support for R&D [research and development], in both the private sector and our research institutions, is critical, as is a national education policy that puts a much higher premium on science and engineering.

Cracking Down on China

Any U.S. manufacturing renaissance must also include leveling the playing field with China. This means cracking down on China's unfair trading practices that include flagrant currency manipulation, illegal export subsidies, rampant piracy of some of America's most sophisticated technologies, and some of the laxest environmental and health and safety regulations in the world.

Cracking down on China's unfair trade practices is not "protectionism." It is a necessary policy response to a set of mercantilist practices that have stolen millions of jobs from America and helped dig the recessionary hole we find ourselves in. If only our presidential candidates—and president!—would get the message.

Reducing the U.S.-China Trade Deficit Should Not Be a Primary U.S. Objective

Steve H. Hanke

Steve H. Hanke is a professor of applied economics at The Johns Hopkins University in Baltimore and a senior fellow at the Cato Institute, a libertarian think tank in Washington, D.C.

The United States has recorded a trade deficit in each year since 1975. This is not surprising because savings in the US have been less than investment.

The trade deficit can be reduced by some combination of lower government consumption, lower private consumption or lower private domestic investment. But you wouldn't know it from listening to the rhetoric of Washington's politicians and special interest groups. Many of them are intent on displaying their mercantilist machismo.

This is unfortunate. A reduction of the trade deficit should not even be a primary objective of federal policy. Never mind. Washington seems to thrive on counter-productive trade "wars" that damage both the US and its trading partners.

The Japanese Example

From the early 1970s until 1995, Japan was an enemy. The mercantilist in Washington asserted that unfair Japanese trading practices caused the US trade deficit and that the US bilateral trade deficit with Japan could be reduced if the yen [Japanese currency] appreciated against the dollar. Washington even tried to convince Tokyo that an ever-appreciating yen would be good for Japan. Unfortunately, the Japanese

Steve H. Hanke, "US Mercantilist Machismo, China Replaces Japan," *Globe Asia*, January 2008. Reprinted at www.freemarketfoundation.com/Hanke/US%20mercantilist%20machismo%20China%20replaces%20Japan%20January%202008.pdf. Reproduced by permission.

complied and the yen appreciated, moving from 360 to the green-back in 1971 to 80 in 1995.

In April 1995, Secretary of the Treasury Robert Rubin belatedly realized that the yen's great appreciation was causing the Japanese economy to sink into a deflationary quagmire. In consequence, the US stopped arm-twisting the Japanese government about the value of the yen and Secretary Rubin began to evoke his now-famous strong-dollar mantra.

But while this policy switch was welcomed, it was too late. Even today, Japan continues to suffer from the mess created by the yen's appreciation. As Japan's economy stagnated, its contribution to the increasing US trade deficit declined, falling from its 1991 peak of almost 60% to about 11% [in 2006].

The China Currency Controversy

While Japan's contribution declined, China's surged from slightly more than 9% in 1990 to almost 28% last year [2007]. With these trends, the Chinese yuan [Chinese dollar] replaced the Japanese yen as the mercantilists' whipping boy.

Interestingly, the combined Japanese-Chinese contribution has actually declined from its 1991 peak of over 70% to only 39% last year [2007]. This hasn't stopped the mercantilists from claiming that the Chinese yuan is grossly undervalued, and that this creates unfair Chinese competition and a US bilateral trade deficit with China.

I was introduced to the Chinese currency controversy five years ago when I appeared as a witness before the US Senate Banking Committee on May 1, 2002. The purpose of those hearings was to determine, among other things, whether China was manipulating its exchange rate.

United States law requires the US Treasury Department [an executive agency responsible for the financial prosperity and security of the United States], in consultation with the International Monetary Fund [an International Organization that oversees global finances], to report bi-yearly as to whether countries—like China—are gaining an "unfair" competitive advantage in international trade by manipulating their currencies.

The US Treasury failed to name China a currency manipulator back in May 2002, and it hasn't done so since then. This isn't too surprising since the term "currency manipulation" is hard to define and, therefore, is not an operational concept that can be used for economic analysis. The US Treasury acknowledged this fact in reports to the US Congress in 2005.

But this fact has not stopped politicians and special interest groups in the United States, and elsewhere, from asserting that China manipulates the yuan. Protectionist from both political parties in the US have threatened to impose tariffs on imported Chinese goods if Beijing does not dramatically appreciate the yuan. These protectionists even claim that China would be much better off if it allowed the yuan to become stronger vis-à-vis the US dollar.

Foreign politicians should stop bashing the Chinese about the yuan's exchange rate.

This is not the first time US special interest have made assertions in the name of helping China. During his first term, Franklin D. Roosevelt delivered on a promise to do something to help silver producers. Using the authority granted by the Thomas Amendment of 1933 and the Silver Purchase Act of 1934, the Roosevelt Administration bought silver. This in addition to bullish rumors about US silver policies, helped push the price of silver up by 128% in the 1932–35 period.

Bizarre arguments contributed mightily to the agitation for high silver prices. One centered on China and the fact that it was on the silver standard. Silver interests asserted that higher silver prices—which would bring with them an appreciation in the yuan—would benefit the Chinese by increasing their purchasing power.

As a special committee of the US Senate reported in 1932, "silver is the measure of their wealth and purchasing power; it serves as a reserve, their bank account. This is wealth that enables such peoples to purchase our exports."

Things didn't work according to Washington's scenario. As the dollar price of silver and of the yuan shot up, China was thrown into the jaws of depression and deflation. In the 1932–34 period, gross domestic product fell by 26% and wholesale prices in the capital city, Nanjing, fell by 20%.

In an attempt to secure relief from the economic hardships imposed by US silver policies, China sought modifications in the US Treasury's silver-purchase program. But its pleas fell on deaf ears. After many evasive replies, the Roosevelt Administration finally indicated on October 12, 1934 that it was merely carrying out a policy mandated by the US Congress.

Realizing that all hope was lost, China was forced to effectively abandon the silver standard on October 14, 1934, though an official statement was postponed until November 3, 1935. This spelled the beginning of the end for Chiang Kai-shek's Nationalist government.

History doesn't have to repeat itself. Foreign politicians should stop bashing the Chinese about the yuan's exchange rate. This would allow the Chinese to focus on important currency and trade issues: making the yuan fully convertible [easily exchanged for other currencies], respecting intellectual property rights and meeting accepted health and safety standards for their exports.

Congress Should Look to American Practices to Solve the Deficit

James A. Dorn

James A. Dorn is a China specialist at the Cato Institute, a libertarian think tank in Washington, D.C., and coeditor of China's Future: Constructive Partner or Emerging Threat?.

A fter several months of relative calm on Capitol Hill about US-China trade relations, leading House [of Representatives] Democrats are making a noise [in 2008]. They are calling on the [George W.] Bush administration to employ "all available tools at its disposal to address China's protracted, large-scale intervention in the foreign exchange markets to maintain an undervalued currency".

Congressional Actions

In a five-page letter [in April 2008, House of Representatives] Ways and Means Committee chairman Charles Rangel, and trade subcommitte chairman Sander Levin called for denying China a larger governance role at the International Monetary Fund [IMF, an international organization that oversees the global financial system] unless Beijing stops intervening in the foreign exchange market. The letter was signed by 15 of the 24 Democratic members of the Ways and Means Committee.

House Democrats see the IMF as an ally in pressuring China to allow faster appreciation of the yuan [Chinese dollar]. They are encouraged, no doubt, by the fund's decision in June [2007] last year to monitor members' exchange-rate policies with an eye towards achieving external stability and preventing fundamentally misaligned exchange rates.

James A. Dorn, "America's Protectionist Drift," *South China Morning Post*, April 4, 2008. Reprinted at www.cato.org/pub_display.php?pub_id=9316. Reproduced by permission.

Under this rubric, China's persistent and large current account surplus, massive foreign exchange reserves and capital controls imply a "fundamentally misaligned" exchange rate, which would compel Beijing to consult the IMF. Mr Rangel wants concrete action to penalise China if it fails to comply with requests to realign its currency.

By a vote of 20 to 1 last summer, the Senate Finance Committee passed the currency exchange rate oversight reform act, hoping to counteract the "unfair trade" practice of maintaining a misaligned currency to gain a competitive advantage. Senator Lindsey Graham crowed: "No longer will the United States sit on the sidelines and allow other nations to gain an unfair advantage. . . . For too long, the game has been rigged against American business." Under the act, if China took no corrective action, the US Treasury could more easily label it a "currency manipulator" and take account of the undervalued yuan in determining duties under anti-dumping laws. Treasury officials would have to consult the IMF, but could recommend changes in governance to penalise China.

China faces increasing inflation and, thus, has an incentive to allow faster appreciation of the yuan, without being pressured by the US.

If Beijing continued to disregard the request for realigning the yuan, the US trade representative would be required to bring the case to the World Trade Organisation [WTO, an international organization that regulates global trade], for dispute settlement consultations.

Although this legislation has not passed Congress, it points to the path the US is likely to take in confronting China—especially the increased role of the IMF. Yet, the IMF has already lost much of its credibility, and countries with large foreign-exchange reserves can safely ignore its advice. It's also unlikely the WTO would chastise a member for its exchange-rate policies.

The US cannot use the IMF to discipline members for failing to revalue their currencies in line with some unknowable "fundamental equilibrium exchange rate". Moreover, America's current-account deficit is not the result of China's undervalued currency, although that may be a contributing factor. The major reason is that US domestic private investment exceeds domestic saving, and a bloated federal government is absorbing domestic saving for redistribution rather than productive investment. Unless the savings-investment gap is closed and the US budget deficit is reduced—by constraining the growth of government and reforming the tax code—American and global imbalances will persist.

Congress ought to be more concerned with excessive government spending and the massive imbalances in social security and Medicare than with the US-Sino [Chinese] bilateral trade deficit and the dollar-yuan exchange rate. The federal budget deficit is expected to grow to more than US$500 billion in the next fiscal year [2009], and the present value of the unfunded liabilities in social security and Medicare now amount to nearly US$43 trillion.

House Democrats have conveniently ignored these problems and chosen to use China as a scapegoat in an election year. China faces increasing inflation and, thus, has an incentive to allow faster appreciation of the yuan, without being pressured by the US and IMF. China's growth is an opportunity for American growth, as well, so Congress would accomplish more by correcting its protectionist drift than trying vainly to reduce China's influence at the IMF and manipulate exchange rates to its liking.

If a new trade strategy is needed, it should be one that recognises the wisdom of philosopher David Hume's [an 18th-century Scottish philosopher and economist] statement in

1742: "Where an open communication is preserved among nations, it is impossible but that the domestic industry of every one must receive an increase from the improvements of the others."

The United States Should Not Blame China for the Trade Deficit

Robert J. Shapiro

Robert J. Shapiro is the director of the Globalization Initiative project at New Democratic Network (NDN), a progressive think tank. He also has served as U.S. under secretary of commerce for economic affairs, and was an economic advisor to former president Bill Clinton and to Al Gore and John Kerry in their presidential campaigns.

As the United States files a major case at the World Trade Organization [WTO, an International Organization that regulates global trade] charging China with wholesale piracy of U.S. intellectual property, especially copyrights covering books, music and videos, let's pause and think about our trade deficit with China. The administration is entirely right to file the case—though a little late, given that it's only our third complaint with the WTO over intellectual property violations since George W. Bush took office, compared to fifteen cases filed at the WTO by the [Bill] Clinton administration in its second term alone. We'll get to why those violations matter economically, but first let's look at an even bigger picture.

The Cause of the U.S.-China Trade Deficit

It may not be politically satisfying, but the truth is, we cannot blame any other country's trade practices for the size of our trade deficit. We run trade deficits for one reason: We consume more than we produce and then purchase the difference from abroad. When China sells paper or t-shirts for less than

Robert J. Shapiro, "Thinking About Our Trade Deficit with China," NDN, April 13, 2007. www.ndn.org/advocacy/globalization/ourtradedeficit.html. © 2006 NDN. Paid for by NDN. NDN is a non-profit 501(c)(4) issue advocacy organization. Reproduced by permission.

they cost to produce and ship them here, it increases our imports of Chinese paper and t-shirts, hurting American workers and companies that still produce them here. But if China charged three times as much, and we bought more paper and t-shirts from American or other foreign suppliers, it could affect the composition of our trade deficit, but not its overall size: That's because the size is locked in by how much we consume of everything, relative to how much we produce of everything.

The only way to reduce the trade deficit is to either consume less—which is what economists mean when they say that the answer is to save more—or to produce more. It used to be the case that the two were closely linked: In order to produce more, you had to invest more, and to invest more, you had to save more (and so consume less). Global capital markets have changed that for the United States, where everyone wants to invest: Now, we can invest more even without consuming less—we just have to borrow the investment funds from foreign savers. There's a big cost down the road, since foreigners end up owning more of our companies and real estate, and then taking home their profits and rent—but at least we get to invest.

[Cracking] down on intellectual property violations by our trading partners [is] the only cost-free way to reduce our trade deficit.

Force China to play fair with her trade policies (if we can, which is often doubtful), and we'll end up importing a little less from China and exporting a little more to China. But unless we also begin to consume less overall or to produce more overall, it won't affect the total trade deficit at all. There is one possible way it could do so—if demand for our exports to China goes up, it may lead to greater production at home to fill the need—and the increase in our production can bring down the trade deficit.

Dealing with Intellectual Property Rights Violations

The one exception to all this is what the administration is finally focusing on—foreign violations of the intellectual property rights of American producers. If we could get China, India, Russia and Brazil (the four biggest offenders) to stop appropriating or pirating our pharmaceuticals, software or music and films, it would directly reduce our trade deficit. Our own consumption wouldn't change, but foreign payments back to U.S. companies would increase, just as if our production had increased and all been exported. Stealing our intellectual property, in short, has the effect of reducing our production (more precisely, taking part of our production and pricing it at nothing), which in turn drives up the trade deficit.

So, now there are two reasons to crack down on intellectual property violations by our trading partners. It's the only cost-free way to reduce our trade deficit, and it should increase the returns and incentives for producing more of it, at a time when globalization and technology make intellectual property a central factor in U.S. economic growth and progress.

One more word on our trade deficit with China: Half of it comes from U.S. companies bringing back products they've produced in China by their Chinese subsidiaries. China's currency is undervalued by all the standard economic measures. But if China does revalue its currency, so its exports become more expensive, it will raise the price of products produced by American companies there for sale here—and by itself can't affect the overall trade deficit.

Protectionism Trade Policies Could Hurt the Global Economy

Daniel Ikenson

Daniel Ikenson is associate director of the Center for Trade Policy Studies at the Cato Institute, a libertarian think tank in Washington, D.C.

The world will [soon] learn whether America's budding protectionism reaches full bloom or is just a passing fancy. The global economy can shake off a failed Doha [Qatar] Round of multilateral trade negotiations without missing two beats. But if the United States turns inward as well, the consequences could be profound and far-reaching.

The U.S. Trend Toward Protectionism

Some would argue that US protectionism is already beyond the budding stage. There has been an explosion in the use of trade remedies in 2007, including the first US antidumping case initiated against Australia in 15 years. . . .

Earlier this year [2007], the United States launched three high-profile complaints against China in the World Trade Organization [WTO, an International Organization that regulates global trade], and reversed its 23-year-old policy of not applying the countervailing duty (or anti-subsidy) law to so-called non-market economies, when it initiated a case against Chinese paper manufacturers in April. And there has been a lot of sabre-rattling in Congress over a host of allegedly unfair Chinese trade practices.

But, by and large, the United States has yet to cross the precipice. Bringing antidumping and countervailing duty cases and launching WTO complaints are all permitted within the

Daniel Ikenson, "A New Protectionism: Dashed Hopes and Perhaps Worse for US Trade Policy," *IPA Review*, October 2007.

global trade rules. Those actions are not necessarily cause for alarm—at least relative to what could be in store in the months ahead.

The Democratic Party, which has grown increasingly hostile towards trade over the past decade, controls the legislature, and thus the policy agenda, for the first time in 12 years.

The primary target of most provocative legislation is China.

President George W. Bush's authority to negotiate trade agreements and present them to Congress for an up-or-down vote (the so-called Fast Track or Trade Promotion Authority) expired in June [2007], and will not be renewed. Completed bilateral trade agreements with South Korea, Colombia, Peru and Panama have been shunted aside to consider, instead, trade legislation that is antagonistic, if not expressly protectionist. Although a few of those bills were crafted mostly for political effect, it is a good bet that some of the nearly two dozen pieces of provocative trade legislation will at least make it to the floors of both chambers of Congress for official votes before the 2008 elections.

As Congress reconvenes in Washington, it is likely to begin moving some of those bills, which include, among other things, provisions that:

- make enforcement of trade agreements systematic and mandatory;

- lower the current evidentiary thresholds for imposing antidumping, anti-subsidy, and China-specific safeguard duties;

- establish a panel of retired federal judges to review adverse WTO decisions and advise Congress on the propriety of those decisions before any steps toward compliance are undertaken;

- forbid the United States from entering into any new trade agreements;

- revoke China's 'normal trade relations' status;

- define and treat currency manipulation as a counter-vailable subsidy;

- require the President to pursue concrete measures to achieve greater trade balance with countries that have persistent trade surpluses with the United States; and,

- expand trade adjustment assistance programmes to cover people who have lost jobs in the services sectors due to outsourcing.

Implicit in this legislation: trade liberalisation is bad, US trade partners cheat, and the folly of America's embrace of globalisation is evidenced by its massive human toll.

Adoption of the kinds of protectionist policies under consideration in the United States would likely have a dramatic, adverse impact on the global economy.

The Effects of Protectionist Policies

The primary target of most provocative legislation is China. But that shouldn't prompt sighs of relief in other countries. Thwarting Chinese imports into the United States is an indirect assault on other countries, particularly those in the Asia-Pacific region. What the US Congress fails to grasp is that many products imported from China comprise value-added materials and labour services provided mostly in other countries. In that regard, the bilateral US trade deficit with China is a meaningless statistic. Yet it fuels the legislative push for action.

Adoption of the kinds of protectionist policies under consideration in the United States would likely have a dramatic, adverse impact on the global economy, with particularly acute

consequences felt in countries that supply China with components, machinery, and raw materials. If the world's largest
consuming nation buys fewer Chinese wares, Chinese factories
won't be buying as much iron ore, bauxite, electronic components, or LCD [liquid crystal display] screens. There is indeed
a bit of Australia, Japan, Korea, and Malaysia in the typical
Chinese cargo container unloaded in Long Beach, California.

Furthermore, legislation that effectively challenges the efficacy and legitimacy of the WTO dispute settlement system
can only lead to a weakening of the multilateral trading system, as other countries are tempted to follow suit and treat
adherence to the rules as optional. Ironically, the Congress is
seeking to beef up US enforcement and prosecutorial capacity
to bring more WTO cases, while it simultaneously considers a
bill that denigrates the WTO process, as well as other bills
containing provisions likely to be WTO-inconsistent.

The WTO system isn't perfect, but it has worked well to
facilitate the growth of trade and investment, while practically
extinguishing the historic tendency towards tit-for-tat trade
wars. Until now, at least.

America's Change of Heart on Trade Policy

Once-giddy expectations for comprehensive international trade
liberalisation at the outset of the Bush Administration have
been downgraded to hoping that the US President is prepared
to veto the slew of anti-trade legislation expected to reach his
desk. Not too long ago, Bush Administration officials spoke
optimistically about a free trade zone 'from Alaska to Tierra
del Fuego', and a world free of industrial tariffs by 2015. The
Administration initiated bilateral trade talks with dozens of
countries as part of its programme of 'competitive
liberalisation', hoping that the momentum that it spurred
would lead to a relatively quick and successful conclusion to
the Doha Round.

But Doha lies in a cryogenic state and it remains to be seen whether the Bush Administration is able—even willing—to hold the line against the impending protectionist offensive. Some in Congress speak of veto-proof majorities (Congress can override a Presidential veto with support from two-thirds of each chamber), which attests to the growing bipartisan nature of skepticism over trade.

Not long ago, Republicans were solidly in the pro-trade camp, while Democrats abandoned the pro-union, anti-trade line with infrequency and at their individual peril. As we enter the spirited US election season, President Bush is likely to be pressured by Republican lawmakers and the party leadership to acquiesce before the rising protectionist tide in an effort to minimise Republican losses in November 2008.

The era of negotiation and accommodation and optimism has yielded to one of confrontation and litigation and skepticism.

It is difficult to pinpoint a specific event that precipitated America's apparent change of heart. It has been more of a drift, perpetuated by a confluence of several factors, including the rise of China, the myth of US manufacturing decline, relentless salesmanship from politicians and media personalities of their mercantilist narratives, widespread disaffection for President Bush and, also, the failure of the Bush Administration to make a convincing, comprehensive case to the American public about the benefits of trade liberalisation.

The Failures of the Bush Administration

That last factor is probably the most significant determinant of the present state of affairs. Had the Administration done a better job of communicating the merits of a liberal trade agenda through its words and actions, the other factors might never have risen to prominence.

But instead, the Bush team opted to politicise the process. They reckoned that with a Republican majority in Congress at the time, the trade agenda could advance without need of much Democratic support. Given the anti-trade sentiments permeating the Democratic caucus, that strategy had virtue, if not merit.

Ultimately, though, that approach alienated important Democrats who now control the congressional trade agenda. And it would be naïve to think that experience doesn't colour their current perspectives on trade policy.

Bush granted steel tariffs to make it easier for certain Republicans in Congress to support trade promotion authority—a move characterised by former US Trade Representative [USTR] Robert Zoellick as 'one step back for two steps forward'. Similar protectionist back-steps were taken to secure support from key Republicans in textile- and farm-states, as well. In that process, the Administration legitimised the claims to exceptional treatment for import-competing industries while preaching the merits of free trade abroad, a hypocrisy that contributed to the poisoned atmosphere surrounding the Doha Round.

The key to achieving greater trade balance without sparking a US recession is not ... protectionist legislation, but [encouraging] Chinese consumption.

The Administration also erred badly in the way it promoted trade agreements. The USTR's office has had a short-sighted tendency to focus on the benefits of trade from an exporter's perspective. A common refrain from the USTR when pitching trade liberalisation is that the United States runs an aggregate trade surplus with the dozen or so countries with which the Administration had concluded bilateral or regional trade agreements—the implication being that strong export growth and minimal import growth constitutes success. But if that's the appropriate metric, it doesn't take much of a leap to conclude that US trade policy is failing given an overall trade deficit approaching $1 trillion.

China's Unfair Trade Practices

That kind of salesmanship—touting exports and downplaying the benefits of imports, which are the source of most of the gains from trade—played into the hands of the mercantilists in Congress, where too many already believe that exports are good, imports are bad, and the trade account is the scoreboard. To them, the large and growing trade deficit is confirmation that the United States is losing at trade. And it is losing, in large measure, because US trade partners are cheating.

In China's case, the purported transgressions include currency manipulation, widespread subsidisation of industry, unfair labour practices, intellectual property theft, opaque market barriers, among others. Some of the allegations have some degree of merit, but not to an extent that comes close to explaining even a fraction of the bilateral deficit.

Allegations of currency manipulation and its adverse impact on the US manufacturing sector have dominated the political discourse this year. As Congress gripes and threatens action, the Chinese Yuan [dollar] continues to appreciate against the US dollar. It is up nearly 8 per cent since the firm dollar peg was abandoned in July 2005. Yet the bilateral deficit continues to rise. It is quite clear that Congress hasn't given much thought to the prospect that a dramatically appreciated Yuan could actually increase the deficit.

The key to achieving greater trade balance without sparking a US recession is not to tax US consumption through protectionist legislation, but to encourage Chinese consumption. That is the essence of what has become known in Washington as the 'Paulson Approach'. Treasury Secretary Henry Paulson has been engaged in dialogue with his Chinese counterparts, trying to foster the kinds of structural changes needed to dissuade excessive thrift there. However, Congress seeks fireworks, not durable solutions.

The Truth About Trade

But why focus on the trade balance at all? Japan has run a trade surplus for decades, but its economy has been stagnant for the better part of the last 15 years. The Germans have a large trade surplus, but double-digit unemployment. The United States has a large and growing trade deficit, but also consistently strong economic growth and an unemployment rate, near all-time lows, of 4.5 per cent.

Still, the trade account as scoreboard metaphor resonates. Americans are told repeatedly that their jobs are being exported to China and India and that the trade deficit is a proxy for job loss. The loss of nearly 3 million US manufacturing jobs during the recession of 2001–2002 is constantly cited as evidence of failed trade policies, even though the US economy has generated 1.8 million net new jobs every year, on average, since 1980, when imports, in real terms, were only 45 per cent of what they are today.

Policymakers have perpetuated a myth that the US manufacturing sector is in decline, which has encouraged further skepticism among Americans about trade. But closer examination reveals not only that US manufacturing is thriving according to every relevant financial yardstick (in 2006, the sector achieved record sales, record profits, record output, and record return on investment), but that it is thriving in large measure because of relatively open US trade policies.

Access to foreign markets has been a crucial component of US manufacturing revenue growth. And access to imported raw materials, components, and capital equipment has helped keep the lid on US manufacturers' costs. In fact, US producers accounted for 55 per cent of total US imports in 2006, which affirms a long-observed relationship in the manufacturing sector: imports and output move in tandem.

It is unlikely that the truth about trade and manufacturing will suddenly prevail upon the political discourse and reverse America's growing skepticism. Not with an election on the horizon [2008]. Perhaps the best to hope for is that some of the pending legislation is made less onerous as it advances through the process, while President Bush does his part to veto legislation that would take the United States, and the world, down a path it would regret.

Organizations to Contact

The editors have compiled the following list of organizations concerned with the issues debated in this book. The descriptions are derived from materials provided by the organizations. All have publications or information available for interested readers. The list was compiled on the date of publication of the present volume; the information provided here may change. Be aware that many organizations take several weeks or longer to respond to inquiries, so allow as much time as possible.

China Daily Information
6/F B3, Thunis Development Mansion, No. 11 Huixin Dongjie
Chaoyang District, Beijing   100029
   PRC
+86(10) 84883300 • fax: +86(10) 84883600
Web site: www.chinadaily.com.cn

China Daily Information operates ChinaDaily.com, one of China's top news portals whose mission is to connect China and the world. The Web site provides up-to-the-minute, in-depth news and information about Chinese politics, economy, culture, entertainment, and lifestyle to millions of online readers. It also covers international news and provides in-depth analysis through columnists, opinions, and editorials. The Web site also contains articles and news reports about U.S.-China trade.

Food and Water Watch
1616 P St. NW, Suite 300, Washington, DC   20036
(202) 683-2500 • fax: (202) 683-2501
E-mail: foodandwater@fwwatch.org
Web site: www.foodandwaterwatch.org

Food and Water Watch is a watchdog group that monitors government standards and oversight of the safety of food and water, challenges the corporate control and abuse of food and water resources, and provides information to the public about these important issues. The Web site contains press releases and alerts concerning the quality and safety of Chinese food imports.

International Trade Administration (ITA)

U.S. Department of Commerce, 1401 Constitution Ave. NW
Washington, DC   20230
(800) 872-8723
Web site: http://trade.gov/index.asp

Part of the U.S. Department of Commerce, ITA's mission is to create prosperity by strengthening the competitiveness of U.S. industry, promoting trade and investment, and ensuring fair trade and compliance with trade laws and agreements. The agency's Web site provides information about U.S. international trade policy, including trade statistics, press releases, speeches, and an online bookstore that provides access to various agency reports and studies. The Web site also includes links to numerous government publications on trading with China.

John L. Thornton China Center

Brookings Institution, 1775 Massachusetts Ave. NW
Washington, DC   20036
(202) 797-6000 • fax: (202) 797-6004
E-mail: brookinfo@brook.edu
Web site: www.brookings.edu/china.aspx

The John L. Thornton China Center is a project of the Brookings Institution, a think-tank that conducts research and education in the areas of foreign policy, economics, government, and the social sciences. The China Center provides timely, independent analyses and policy recommendations to help U.S. and Chinese leaders address key long-term challenges, both in terms of U.S.-China relations and China's internal development. The organization's Web site features numerous publications on China, including, *China's Economic Decisionmakers* and *Facing Protectionism Generated by Trade Disputes: China's Post-WTO Blues.*

United Nations Conference on Trade and Development (UNCTAD)

Palais des Nations, 8-14, Av. de la Paix, Geneva 10   1211
  Switzerland
+41-22-917-5809 • fax: +41-22-917-0051
E-mail: info@unctad.org
Web site: www.unctad.org/

UNCTAD was established by the United Nations (UN) to help integrate developing countries into the world economy. UNCTAD has addressed China's growing importance in the world economy in a number of informative analyses and publications, including: *Key Issues in China's Economic Transformation, Trade and Development Report 2005* (which examines the underlying forces of China as a key player in the world economy) and *Trade and Development Report 2006* (which discusses the implications of different ways of correcting the existing global imbalances).

U.S. Census Bureau: Foreign Trade Statistics

U.S. Census Bureau, 4600 Silver Hill Rd.
Washington, DC   20233
E-mail: pio@census.gov
Web site: www.census.gov/foreign-trade/www/

Part of the U.S. Census Bureau, the Foreign Trade Statistics division is a U.S. government agency that compiles and disseminates statistical information about U.S. trade. Among other publications, the division produces the *Guide to Foreign Trade Statistics*, which offers statistics on imports and exports on a country-by-country basis.

The US-China Business Council, Inc. (USCBC)

1818 N St. NW, Suite 200, Washington, DC   20036
(202) 429-0340 • fax: (202) 775-2476
Web site: www.uschina.org

The US-China Business Council, Inc. (USCBC) is a private, nonprofit organization of more than 250 American corporations that do business with China. Its mission is to expand the

United States' commercial relationship with China to the benefit of the U.S. economy. USCBC advocates a balanced approach to trade with China—one that expands opportunities while identifying and removing trade barriers. The organization's Web site features a wide variety of statistical and policy reports, analyses, and other publications relevant to U.S-China trade relations.

U.S.-China Economic and Security
Review Commission (USCC)
444 North Capitol St. NW, Suite 602, Washington, DC   20001
(202) 624-1407
E-mail: contact@uscc.gov
Web site: www.uscc.gov

The U.S.-China Economic and Security Review Commission was created in 2000 to monitor, investigate, and submit to the U.S. Congress an annual report on the national security implications of the bilateral trade and economic relationship of the United States and the People's Republic of China, and to provide recommendations, where appropriate, to Congress for legislative and administrative action. The Commission's Web site offers information concerning the bilateral trade and economic relationship between the United States and China and outlines legislative and administrative action taken by Congress.

U.S.-China Policy Foundation
316 Pennsylvania Ave. SE, Suite 201–202
Washington, DC   20003
(202) 547-8615 • fax: (202) 547-8853
E-mail: uscpf@uscpf.org
Web site: www.uscpf.org

The U.S.-China Policy Foundation is a non-partisan, non-profit, non-advocacy educational organization devoted to broadening awareness of China and U.S.-China relations in the Washington, D.C., policy community. The group publishes a bi-annual report called the *Washington Journal of Modern*

China and a newsletter titled *U.S.-China Policy Review,* and it also produces *China Forum,* an educational television program devoted exclusively to China.

U.S. Consumer Product Safety Commission (CPSC)

4330 East West Highway, Bethesda, MD   20814
(301) 504-7923 • fax: (301) 504-0124
Web site: www.cpsc.gov

The U.S. Consumer Product Safety Commission is charged with protecting the public from unreasonable risks of serious injury or death from more than 15,000 types of consumer products under the agency's jurisdiction. The Commission's Web site includes numerous publications relating to Chinese imports, China's efforts to improve the quality and safety of its imports, and various recalls by the Commission of products manufactured in China and elsewhere.

U.S. Food and Drug Administration (FDA)

5600 Fishers Lane, Rockville, MD   20857-0001
(888) 463-6332
Web site: www.fda.gov/

The U.S. Food and Drug Administration (FDA) is responsible for protecting the public health by ensuring the safety, efficacy, and security of human and veterinary drugs, biological products, medical devices, our nation's food supply, cosmetics, and products that emit radiation. The FDA Web site contains information—testimony, news articles, transcripts of press conferences, reports, and other publications—relevant to the issue of Chinese food and drug imports, China's trade policies, and actions being taken by the U.S. government to ensure safe imports.

World Bank

1818 H St. NW, Washington, DC   20433
(202) 473-1000 • fax: (202) 477-6391
Web site: www.worldbank.org

The World Bank seeks to reduce poverty and improve the standards of living of poor people around the world. It promotes sustainable growth and investments in developing countries through loans, technical assistance, and policy guidance. The World Bank Web site contains a section on China that offers a variety of resources on the country and its economic rise to power. These include a country overview, a country brief (which summarizes recent developments, future challenges, and Bank assistance to China), and numerous free publications. One such publication is *China Quarterly Update*, which reports on the country's economic status.

World Trade Organization (WTO)
Centre William Rappard, Rue de Lausanne 154
Geneva 21 CH-1211
  Switzerland
+41-22-739-5111 • fax: +41-22-731-4206
E-mail: enquiries@wto.org
Web site: www.wto.org

The World Trade Organization (WTO) is a global international organization that establishes rules of trade between nations. It also is a forum where countries can negotiate trade agreements and settle trade disputes. Two WTO agreements have been negotiated and signed by the bulk of the world's trading nations and ratified in their parliaments. The goal of these agreements is to help producers of goods and services, exporters, and importers conduct their business. WTO publishes trade statistics, research and analysis, studies, reports, and the journal *World Trade Review*. The WTO Web site includes a page devoted to China and that country's participation in WTO since it joined in 2001.

Bibliography

Books

Barton V. Celone — *China-United States Trade: Inextricably Intertwined?*, Hauppauge, NY: Nova Science Publishers, 2008.

Center for Strategic and International Studies and the Institute for International Economics — *China, the Balance Sheet: What the World Needs to Know Now About the Emerging Superpower*, New York: PublicAffairs, 2006.

Ted C. Fishman — *China, Inc.: How the Rise of the Next Superpower Challenges America and the World*, New York: Scribner, 2006.

Rob Gifford — *China Road: A Journey into the Future of a Rising Power*, New York: Random House Trade Paperbacks, 2008.

W. John Hoffman et al. — *China Into the Future: Making Sense of the World's Most Dynamic Economy*, Hoboken, NJ: Wiley, 2007.

James Kynge — *China Shakes the World: A Titan's Rise and Troubled Future—and the Challenge for America*, New York: Mariner Books, 2007.

Nicholas R. Lardy — *Integrating China Into the Global Economy*, Washington, DC: Brookings Institution Press, 2002.

Michael L. Levin   *The Next Great Clash: China and Russia vs. the United States*, Westport, CT: Praeger Security International, 2007.

Constantine C. Menges   *China: The Gathering Threat*, Nashville, TN: Thomas Nelson, 2005.

Robyn Meredith   *The Elephant and the Dragon: The Rise of India and China and What It Means for All of Us*, New York: W.W. Norton, 2007.

Peter Navarro   *The Coming China Wars: Where They Will Be Fought and How They Can Be Won*, Upper Saddle River, NJ: FT Press, 2006.

Supachai Panitchpakdi and Mark L. Clifford   *China and the WTO: Changing China, Changing World Trade*, Hoboken, NJ: Wiley, 2002.

Oded Shenkar   *The Chinese Century: The Rising Chinese Economy and Its Impact on the Global Economy, the Balance of Power, and Your Job*, Philadelphia: Wharton School Publishing, 2006.

Susan L. Shirk   *China, Fragile Superpower: How China's Internal Politics Could Derail Its Peaceful Rise*, New York: Oxford University Press, 2007.

Yee Wong and Ketki Sheth   *US-China Trade Disputes: Rising Tide, Rising Stakes*, Washington, DC: Institute for International Economics, 2006.

Stephen J. Yates   *How Trade with China Benefits Americans*, Washington, DC: The Heritage Foundation, 2002.

Periodicals

Mary Amiti and Caroline Freund   "China's Export Boom," *Finance and Development*, September 2007. www.imf.org/external/pubs/ft/fandd/2007/09/amiti.htm.

The Associated Press   "China to Enact New Product Safety Rules in Bid to Restore Its Reputation," *International Herald-Tribune*, March 5, 2008. www.iht.com/articles/ap/2008/03/05/asia/AS-GEN-China-Tainted-Products.php.

Elizabeth Becker   "Bush Rejects Labor's Call to Punish China," *New York Times*, April 29, 2004. http://query.nytimes.com/gst/fullpage.html?res=9903EEDA163DF93AA15757C0A9629C8B63.

Ben Blanchard   "China Says Product Safety Push a Complete Success," *Reuters*, January 14, 2008. www.reuters.com/article/topNews/idUSPEK35562720080114?feedType=RSS&feedName=topNews.

Business Week   "Imports From China Aren't Pricier—Yet," March 27, 2006. www.businessweek.com/magazine/content/06_13/b3977052.htm.

China Daily "Many Americans Can't Live Without China Goods," July 22, 2007. www.chinadaily.com.cn/china/2007-07/22/content_5441067.htm.

Evan Clark and Kristi Ellis "Bush Called to Action on China Imports," *Women' Wear Daily*, February 13, 2006.

Pete Engardio "'Substantial Benefits' from China Trade? A New Economic Study Says the U.S. Gains Plenty from Its Commerce with China, While Admitting that Disruptions Are Also Significant," *Business Week Online*, February 8, 2006. www.businessweek.com/bwdaily/dnflash/feb2006/nf2006028_2804_db039.htm.

Global Agenda "China's New Trade Horizons, China's Trade with the World: China Still Cares Most About Exports to Europe and America," February 9, 2007.

Pallavi Gogoi "China's Growing Exports: Food and Fear," *Business Week Online*, May 23, 2007. www.businessweek.com/bwdaily/dnflash/content/may2007/db20070523_447291.htm.

Neil C. Hughes "A Trade War with China?" *Foreign Affairs*, July/August 2005. www.foreignaffairs.org/20050701faessay84407/neil-c-hughes/a-trade-war-with-china.html.

Joseph Kahn	"Can China Reform Itself?" *New York Times*, July 8, 2007. www.nytimes.com/2007/07/08/weekin review/08kahn.html?_r=2&fta=y&oref =slogin&oref=slogin.
David J. Lynch	"Do Cheap Chinese Goods Have to Mean Trade-Off in Quality?" *USA Today*, July 2, 2007. www.usatoday.com/money/world/ 2007-07-02-china-risks_N.htm.
Hisane Masaki	"China Passes Us as Top Japan Trade Partner," *Pacific Shipper*, April 27, 2007.
Bob Pisani	"China Imports Costing More: Days of 'Cheap Items' Over?" *CNBC*, February 15, 2008. www.cnbc.com/id/ 23182494?__source=RSS*tag*&par =RSS.
Henry Rosemont, Jr.	"Is China a Threat?" *Foreign Policy in Focus*, Feburary 7, 2008. www.fpif.org/fpiftxt/4945.
Robert J. Samuelson	"China's Trade Time Bomb," *Washington Post*, May 8, 2007. www.washingtonpost.com/wp-dyn/ content/article/2007/05/08/AR2007 050801580.html.
Laura Smith-Spark	"Chinese Product Scares Prompt US Fears," *BBC News*, July 10, 2007. http://news.bbc.co.uk/2/hi/americas/ 6275758.stm.

Joseph Stiglitz   "First Japan, Now China Is the Cul-
                       prit," *The Guardian*, October 15,
                       2003. www.guardian.co.uk/world/
                       2003/oct/15/usa.comment.

Jyoti Thottam   "The Growing Dangers of China
                       Trade," *TIME*, June 28, 2007.
                       www.time.com/time/magazine/article/
                       0,9171,1638436,00.html.

Todd Wallack   "Drug Makers Stick by China," *Bos-
                       ton Globe*, March 14, 2008.
                       www.boston.com/business/healthcare/
                       articles/2008/03/14/drug_makers
                       _stick_by_china/.

Elizabeth Weise   "FDA Limits Chinese Food Additive
and Julie Schmit   Imports," *USA Today*, April 30, 2007.
                       www.usatoday.com/money/industries/
                       2007-04-30-chinese-imports-usat_
                       N.htm.

Index